Experimental Fiction

Also Available from Bloomsbury

The Creative Screenwriter: Exercises to Expand Your Craft, Dr Craig
Batty and Zara Waldeback
The Post-War British Literature Handbook, Katharine Cockin
The Modernism Handbook, Philip Tew
Bending Genre: Essays on Creative Nonfiction, Margot Singer
Maverick Screenwriting: A Manual for the Adventurous Screenwriter,
Josh Golding

Experimental Fiction

An Introduction for Readers and Writers

Julie Armstrong

Bloomsbury Academic
An imprint of Bloomsbury Publishing Plc

B L O O M S B U R Y
LONDON · NEW DELHI · NEW YORK · SYDNEY

Bloomsbury Academic
An imprint of Bloomsbury Publishing Plc

50 Bedford Square
London
WC1B 3DP
UK

1385 Broadway
New York
NY 10018
USA

www.bloomsbury.com

**BLOOMSBURY and the Diana logo are
trademarks of Bloomsbury Publishing Plc**

First published 2014
Reprinted 2014

British Library Cataloguing-in-Publication Data
A catalogue record for this book is available from the British Library.

ISBN: HB: 978-1-4411-8908-0
PB: 978-1-4411-3057-0
ePDF: 978-1-4411-2871-3
ePUB: 978-1-4411-0729-9

Library of Congress Cataloging-in-Publication Data
A catalog record for this book is available from the Library of Congress.

Typeset by Integra Software Services Pvt. Ltd
Printed and bound in Great Britain

For my Creative Writing students, past and present, at MMU Cheshire

Preface and Contents

Who the book is intended for and why

This book is for writers and readers of fiction, especially those who are studying, or have an interest in, experimental literary works. The aim is to enrich readers' knowledge, understanding and appreciation of such works and to enable writers to heighten their powers of imagination whilst developing their craft.

The history of experimental writing, from modernism to the Beats, to postmodernism and beyond, will be traced. In addition, *Experimental Fiction* will analyse why the twenty-first century is a time ripe for change for the reader and the writer.

How the book is organized

Experimental Fiction: An Introduction for Readers and Writers has an Introduction, four sections – Modernism, Beats, Postmodernism, A New Era Dawning – and a Conclusion.

Alongside the historical discussion of each movement, at the end of each chapter there are creative writing exercises designed to stimulate writing experimentation and to introduce techniques which will help learning in terms of the practice of creative writing. References for further reading are also listed. Each section has an introduction.

The conclusion will pose, and hope to find answers to, the following questions:

Having read *Experimental Fiction: An Introduction for Readers and Writers* and completed the exercises, readers and writers will be better informed and more skilful creative writing practitioners.

Acknowledgements

I would like to thank the following colleagues who have kindly supported me in the writing of this book: Ms Carola Boehm, Mr John Deeney, Mr Terry Fox, Dr Robert Graham, Professor Dick Hartley, Ms Angi Holden, Dr Meriel Lland, Professor Berthold Schoene, Ms Jo Selley, Ms Bev Steven, Professor Michael Symmons Roberts and Dr Jane Turner. Many thanks are also due to the team at Bloomsbury: Mark Richardson, Avinash Singh and, in particular, editor David Avital for his vision and rigorous reading of the manuscript.

I would like to thank my Creative Writing students, especially Context 1, 2 and Historical Perspectives students; this book is for you.

Introduction

What does experimental mean?

The word *experimental* is a contested and historically contingent term when applied to fiction. Many readers, writers and critics are unsure about giving fiction the label *experimental*, and as a consequence, there are many questions that need to be fully considered before the label can be applied to literary works. For example, if a writer is creating work in accordance with *new* – not pre-established – conventions of writing, can this fiction be classified as experimental? How can the actual experiment in a piece of unconventional writing be defined? Does fiction which expresses the writer's restlessness with form and content be characterized as experimental? Does what was once labelled *experimental* in one historical period become mainstream fiction in another? Is *experimental* simply a label which identifies the next trend in fiction? Is fiction deemed experimental at the time of writing, or is it established as such by later generations?

Any new writing will owe something to the past and also something to the future in the shaping of ideologies and styles. However, it can be said, the novel is often a product of its time and place. Although, experimental literary works become comprehensible after their unfamiliar structures, forms and content have been conventionalized over time.

It can be acknowledged that there are writers throughout history whose intention is to experiment and create fiction that sets out to break new ground and deviate from traditional realist fiction. Virginia Woolf, for example, declared in her diary that she sought to experiment with her craft and, as a result, she discovered a *new* form for a *new* novel. Jack Kerouac also set out to experiment with his writing and to produce work that contested mainstream, middle-class America. He felt that his writing could not be fully realized through existing traditional novel conventions; they would simply not allow him to tell the story he wanted to tell. By creating his own *rules* or *essentials*, as he referred to them, Kerouac did not produce novels but a *new* prose-narrative form. He used technical devices of epic poetry, which, together with his spontaneous prose, revitalized his writing and resulted in the poetic sprawl *On the Road*.

And yet, it can also be noted that there are other writers who produce *new* works by simply expressing their own, often idiosyncratic personalities, in response to the internal and external worlds they inhabit. There are also writers who are creating works in order to make sense of the world and their place in it, and in so doing, they produce works which depart from tradition realist fiction, a form considered to be too restricting to express some writers' thoughts and ideas. As a consequence, they create new forms, styles and genres of literary work. In addition, there are writers who consciously react against traditional realist fiction with the intention of creating work which will bring about self-realization and change in people's lives, and in so doing, they too establish new forms and content. All of the above writers will be explored in this book.

What are the concerns of experimental writers?

The concerns of individual writers are not always explicit. However, some writers have written essays or diaries or given interviews voicing their preoccupations and citing what their intentions are when creating fiction that opposes traditional realist fiction. Jack Kerouac, for example, stated in numerous interviews that he was preoccupied with writing that had feeling as opposed to craft. He favoured a spontaneous, improvised style, like jazz, a style that was fast, mad, confessional and suited the bohemian content of his work. Gertrude Stein conducted experiments to access the subconscious in order to research into the process of automatic writing. Later, she converted the data into *new* literary fiction. Other contemporary writers, such as the late Scottish-born author Iain Banks, created fiction considered to be thought experiments. In such works, fiction is a vehicle for a writer to investigate ideas and concepts – for example, the Culture series of fiction, which centres around the Culture, a semi-anarchist utopia, consisting of humanoid races managed by advanced artificial intelligence. The main themes of the novels, such as *The Player of Games* and *The State of the Art*, are the dilemmas that an idealistic hyper-power faces in dealing with civilizations that do not share its ideals and behaviour.

Jeanette Winterson has written about her desire to create fiction that addresses twenty-first-century needs. Indeed, many experimental writers, for example, William Gibson and Jon McGregor, despite being different, are both seeking to create new forms, techniques, content and styles to enable them to express what they want to express through their writing. They are looking for *new* ways to tell the *new* stories that they wish to tell. More traditional forms, styles and techniques are too restricting, simply not suited to the ideas and content they wish to explore.

Maybe it is important to seek out an author's intention when writing a particular fiction in order to gain a richer understanding of the text? Maybe the fiction should stand alone? These are questions to be considered.

What is experimental fiction?

Some critics consider experimental fiction to be literary works that are in direct opposition to traditional realist works, whilst there are others who think that experimental fiction is inherently concerned with innovation and risk-taking. This leads to a further set of questions. Do writers set out to self-identify as experimental or are they responding to the changing social, economic, political and cultural times in which they are living? Therefore, is this fiction merely a reflection of these changing times and events or can it be classified as experimental fiction? How have/are writers related/relating to their lifetimes? Are they reflecting ideologies or rejecting them? To reject ideologies, do new techniques have to be invented and employed? And what counts as risk-taking, challenging, new and controversial in the world of fiction?

Firstly, in the hope of answering these questions, it is necessary to understand the differences between traditional realist fiction and fiction that deviates from this model – fiction that can be referred to as experimental.

What are the differences between traditional realist fiction and experimental fiction?

To answer this question, it is imperative to outline what each form of fiction is attempting to achieve.

Traditional realist fiction is attempting to

Reproduce the *real* world in the imagined world of fiction
Create an authenticity of the experience the fiction is attempting to
    portray
Convey a recognizable time scheme
Evoke a vivid sense of place
Have a clear hierarchy of discourses controlled be a privileged central
    voice
Display a coherent explanation of actions
Demonstrate immediacy
Entertain the reader
Set out a plausible sequence of events
Develop credible characters
Produce convincing dialogue
Utilize steadily rising tension and conflict
Engage a reader's emotions and bring about empathy
Bring about closure

Experimental fiction is attempting to

Destabilize the real world
Subvert a sense of the *normal*
Introduce debates about the status of the text and the act of writing
Present different world views
Have free playing voices none of which is privileged
Engage with the moving play of signifiers to construct endless cycles
    of meaning
Employ intrusion into the text by the narrator and/or author
Experiment with form and typography
Develop new ways of seeing
Apply multiple discourses
Mix and/or subvert genres
Provoke the reader to consider ideas and concepts
Imagine alternative realities
Use metaphoric qualities
Engage the reader on an intellectual/philosophical level
Deny closure

As can be seen from these two models, there are differences, often opposing, in terms of what writers of traditional realist fiction and writers of experimental fiction are setting out to achieve; it is therefore useful to acknowledge these differences in terms of our role as readers, if not necessarily in terms of our role as writers.

Narrative is very appealing to readers; this is because it offers simplicity and predictability, which is comforting, unlike experimental fiction, which can be unpredictable, random and confusing. Experimental fiction departs from conventional expectations or Aristotelian principles: that a novel has a beginning, middle and an end, with steadily rising action and conflict that builds to a climax and then resolves – a closed text. These basic characteristics of traditional realist literature, which readers have been taught throughout their education, can be quickly and easily determined to enjoy engagement with a text. This is not the case for experimental fiction. Therefore, a reader's response is sometimes one of frustration and even anger, leading to confusion and disengagement, as experimental works subvert expectations. And yet, experimental fiction is more like *real* life, in that *real* life is tangled, non-linear and complex; it refuses to be packaged into simplistic plots. Experimental works make more and new, sometimes baffling, demands on the reader. So why read experimental fiction?

Why read experimental fiction?

It can be argued that for their work and ideas to evolve and become more imaginative, writers need to move out of their comfort zone and challenge themselves by reading work that challenges them. If everything a writer reads is accessible and familiar, then their writing will become one dimensional and lack vitality. A *real* writer and reader is someone who does not put limits on themselves because to do so stunts growth. Writers who are aware that fiction is capable of doing much more than simply telling a story will become more accomplished, self-aware, insightful practitioners. In addition, by reading experimental fiction, a reader's views on story telling will be revised and they will become more sophisticated readers, ones who have the tools and vocabulary to enjoy a richer, more diverse experience of fiction, which can be very inspiring and rewarding.

How does a reader approach experimental fiction?

When reading as a writer of any fiction, a reader needs to look at how the writing works in terms of craft, form, content and techniques. An awareness of the methods, procedures and strategies writers use can enhance the experience of reading and make it liberating, leading to a fuller understanding of fiction. If a reader is deconstructing fiction that has subverted conventional forms and practices, it is important that a new way of deconstructing work is employed. Clearly, the *old* way of approaching *new* texts is inappropriate. Readers need to engage with experimental fiction in ways in which they are not familiar; therefore, a different set of reading strategies are required for readers to read, interrogate and interpret texts.

Most literary criticism prior to the 1950s was author-centred until a number of critics began to argue that attention should be focused on the text and not on the author. In his 1968 polemic *Death of the Author*, Roland Barthes claimed that it is language that speaks, not the author, and that the text leads a separate existence and the multiplicity of meanings which make up a text is focused on the reader, not the author. Barthes argued that there are two types of texts: writerly and readerly. In writerly, the reader is active. The work is non-linear, open and plural, and allows for play and invention, inviting readers to become participants in the production of meaning: an experimental work. In readerly, the reader is passive. The work is linear, closed. There is often a resolution: a traditional realist work.

Fundamentally, a reader approaching experimental fiction needs to suspend their *autopilot* expectations and discover *new* ways of seeing. Readers are required to become more active and less passive. There is often a denial of, even an attack on, a single unified meaning, and a move away from closure. Experimental fiction, whose aim is not necessarily to tell a story, is often ambiguous and challenges artistic principles; clearly it is writing that has different preoccupations from traditional works and these need to be acknowledged and understood.

What criteria can be used for reading as a writer of experimental fiction?

There are many fiction writing handbooks that demonstrate how a writer can read as a writer of traditional realist fiction – that is, by analysing the skills and techniques used by authors in order to develop and enhance their own craft of writing – but this is not the case for writers and readers of experimental fiction. It is intended that this book will address the imbalance by providing a tool that will enable writers of experimental fiction to develop their craft too. In addition, both readers and writers will discover insights and gain a deeper understanding and appreciation of literary works.

Readers and writers of experimental fiction have to take on a different mindset; they cannot approach experimental fiction in the same way that they approach traditional realist fiction. Indeed, the mindset readers and writers adopt will change over time as fiction inevitably does. As society changes, so do literary works, subverting their own structural and formal bases, altering our perceptions of what fiction and writing is, and can be. Lecturer in English and American Studies Tim Woods says, 'What we think of the novel has lost its credibility – it no longer tells us what we feel to be the truth as we try to keep track of ourselves. There's no point in pushing ahead with fiction ...' (Woods, 1999, Beginning Postmodernism, p. 51). But, if fiction is exhausted, if it is impossible to write an original work, then surely out of this debate there emerges fiction which is concerned with these very notions and its own status.

At this moment in time, what criteria may writers and readers consider when they are deconstructing experimental fiction?

By no means is this list exclusive, but these are some points readers and writers can consider when reading and writing experimental fiction.

Checklist for deconstructing experimental fiction

Does the work subvert some, or all, of the intentions of traditional realist fiction?

Does the work engage with contemporary debates, for example, debates concerning science, culture, politics? How? Why?

Is the work seeking to challenge our intellect and/or question our assumptions regarding fiction?

Are there patterns, repetition, rhythm, gaps between words or phrases, sites of tension and intensity within the fiction? If so, what is their effect?

Is it a work that sets up its own rules while subverting the conventions according to which readers have understood what constitutes a work of literature?

Is the work rejecting rigid boundaries – thinking outside the page?

Does the text unsettle the limitations of genre and convention, subvert familiarity?

Is the fiction drawing the reader's attention away from the story to the act of story telling itself? How? Why? What is the effect?

How does the work articulate emotional states?

What is the structure, mood of the fiction?

How is language being used?

Are their gaps and/or silences within the work? Is the reader required to fill them?

How is punctuation and syntax used?

Is there a mixture of fact and fiction? If, so, why? What purpose does it serve?

Does the work destabilize the real world? How? Why? What is the effect?

Is there author intrusion? What impact does this have upon the reading of the work?

Does the work experiment with form and typography?

Does the work mix and/or subvert genres?

Is there a denial of closure, simply flickering of meanings?

It is hoped that this book will open the eyes of readers and writers to the multiplicity of experimental fiction that is available for them to enjoy, and to prompt those who are interested to engage with further lines of inquiry. It is worth noting that the world is constantly changing and contemporary writing will inevitably change to reflect these changes. Nothing stays the same for long.

Section One

When Was/What Was Modernity(ism)?

When was modernity?

The period of modernity emerged in Europe and the United States between 1880 and 1950, although it may be questionable whether modernity has ended, something that will be explored later in the postmodern section of this book.

Specifically, Virginia Woolf noted December 1910 as a period of change, when, in her view, the character of human beings altered, of particular significance being the roles of women. The period saw demonstrations in London by the suffragettes. Indeed, 1910 was a turbulent time in history, a time which made a break with previous tradition and history. The year witnessed a general election and the death of Edward VII, which marked the beginning of the Georgian Age.

The exhibition *Manet and the Post-Impressionists* was opened by Woolf's friend, the British artist and critic Roger Fry, at the Grafton Galleries in London. 'Post-Impressionism' was a term coined by Fry to describe the development of art since Monet; it was not a formal style or movement, but more of a negative attitude towards Impressionism. This eclectic group of artists were working in a different way from their predecessors by extending Impressionism, rejecting its limitations to focus more on emotional, symbolic, spiritual, intellectual and structural elements of their work. Although continuing to use vivid colour, thick application of paint, distinctive brush strokes and real-life subject matter, they broke free from naturalism to emphasize geometric shapes to make the form more abstract. Each artist took an aspect of Impressionism and exaggerated it, pushing previous ideas into new directions. For example, Vincent van Gogh used exceptionally vibrant paint with a renewed sense of energy and emotion. Georges Seurat took the 'broken' brushwork and developed this technique into lots of tiny coloured dots, known as pointillism. Paul Gauguin incorporated symbolism into his paintings. And Paul Cezanne extended separation of colour into separation of whole planes of colour. The exhibition received a mixed reaction, one of admiration, shock, disbelief and mockery. Woolf was inspired by the artists' techniques, especially those concerned with the use of colour, brushwork, perspective, composition, light and shade.

During this time, painters such as Kandinsky and Klee were producing a *new* kind of artistic practice. Kandinsky was credited with producing the first purely abstract work, whereas Klee was influenced by surrealism and incorporated signs, symbols, images and metaphors into his paintings. His work was considered to be a form of writing. Indeed, Klee refused to make a clear distinction between art and writing.

In 1913, there was the ground-breaking *Armory Show* organized by the Association of American Painters and Sculptors, the first exhibition of modern art in America; it was the first time the phrase 'avant-garde' was used to describe painting and sculpture. The show represented a search for new beauty, new versions of truth and a new way of seeing and was said to have shaken the world whilst attracting 87,000 visitors in New York before moving on to Chicago. The most controversial work was Marcel Duchamp's *Nude Descending a Staircase*, an oil painting which depicted a semi-abstract human figure in brown, assembled in such a way as to suggest rhythm and movement.

In May of the same year, there was also the shocking premiere *Le Sacre Du Printemps*, a ballet and orchestral concert work by Igor Stravinsky written for Serge Diaghilev, the creator of the Ballet Russes, a company which revolutionized dance and commissioned scores which shaped twentieth-century music. Diaghilev was searching for a total art form, one that was a move away from the confines of convention and morality of the nineteenth century, an avant-garde sensibility articulated in the writings of the philosopher Friedrich Nietzsche, who advocated a rebirth of modern society that Diaghilev, Stravinsky and the dancer and choreographer Valslav Nijinsky sought to portray in *Le Sacre*. The score experimented with rhythm, metre and tonality so that the music was dissonant and odd. The choreography represented a shift away from classical ballet: sharp angles of the body, rather than smooth curves, flexed feet instead of pointed toes. The score and choreography, coupled with the subject matter, a pagan celebration in which a virgin sacrifices herself to the god of spring, conveyed nihilism and chaos and almost caused a riot when it was first performed in Paris in 1913.

Although some artists and critics considered 1910 to be the year of change, others, notably Ezra Pound, declared 1922 to be the year of a new age; this was the time James Joyce completed *Ulysses* and T. S. Eliot published *The Wasteland*. According to Kevin Jackson, author of *Constellations of Genius, 1922: Modernism Year One*, these two works have become the 'twin peaks of modernist literature' (Jackson, p. 12). *Ulysses* and *The Wasteland* have been described by Jackson as 'complex works, full of extensive and strange learning, and they demand a degree of attention far higher than that which the average browser is generally willing to give' (Jackson, p. 13). Undoubtedly, this was a time when realist fiction and literary conventions were being dramatically challenged, not just by Joyce and T. S. Eliot, but by many other writers too; for example, Wyndham Lewis published his experimental prose *Tarr*. In this work, Lewis experimented with punctuation, introducing 'paintery strokes' into literature, an equals sign between sentences. Franz Kafka meanwhile wrote visionary yet nightmarish fiction addressing anxieties and changes occurring in the twentieth century, citing Darwin and Nietzsche as his influences. He explored themes of alienation in works such as *The Metamorphosis* (1912).

The year 1922 was remarkable:

Newspapers told of the final collapse of the Ottoman Empire, the end
of British Liberalism with the crushing defeat by the Conservatives at
the end of 1922...In the world of the arts, Dada was put to rest; and
Proust died. (Jackson, p. 16)

Although the First World War (1914–18) brought about significant
technological change, 1922 heralded the birth of mass media. In 1922,
the first facsimile image was sent by telephone line; in addition, there
was the launch of the BBC and the wide circulation of films, with Alfred
Hitchcock directing his first film and the likes of Charlie Chaplin and
Rudolph Valentino being adored by the masses. In 1922,

...there was a frenzy of innovation. Modern linguistic philosophy
can be dated from the publication of Wittgenstein's *Tractatus
Logico-Philosophicus* that year. Modern anthropology began with
the triumphant publication of Malinowski's *Argonauts Of The
Western Pacific*. Kandinsky and Klee joined the Bauhaus...Louis
Armstrong...launched himself as the greatest performer in the
history of jazz. African-American culture came of age with the
first major manifestations of what became known as the Harlem
Renaissance...(Jackson, p. 17)

Whether the actual date of change was 1910 or 1922, there is little doubt
that the beginning of the twentieth century challenged the ways the world
was perceived and transformed beliefs of what art and criticism could be.
The work of artists such as Cezanne and Picasso looked at things from
more than one perspective, provoking the questions: Is this what I see?
Is the artist's function to convey an idea? What makes good art? So, what
brought about this shift in worldview? And what was modernity?

What was modernity?

In his book *Modernism*, Leigh Wilson says that modernity was the
'the events, forces, practices and innovations which, from the late
eighteenth century onwards, created the world, and the worldview,

of the West' (Wilson, 2007, p. 55). As the ordered, stable worldview of the nineteenth century shifted to become more complex and chaotic, the spirit of the time became one of contradiction, angst, rootlessness, disorientation, urban dislocation and, yet, optimism, making the world *new*. Indeed, a phrase that encapsulates this time was *making new*. Modernity then expressed modern life as a break from the past and its classical traditions; it was a condition of being in the modern world, a time of innovation and the rise of capitalism, when a *new* world emerged and a faster-paced existence came into being, one that was very different from that of the traditional Victorians. In part, it was the Industrial Revolution and its fallout that

> constructed modernity … the explosion in population experienced at this time, and the movement of large numbers of people from rural to urban areas to work in the new 'manufactories', eventually forced governments to begin to take responsibilities for the well-being of their citizens through the provision of sanitation, housing and, eventually, education and medical care. (as above, p. 56)

The First World War was also attributed with a shift in the *way* the world was observed, which led to numerous cultural, social and technological advances; these advances had implications for developments in science, communication systems and the growth of urbanism. There were rapid advancements in biological sciences; these heralded significant results in terms of medical practice, which evolved from a primitive to a more sophisticated, enlightened practice, with the use of anaesthetics and a growth in surgical techniques and preventative treatments. Further to this, experiments in electricity led to the discovery of X-rays and radioactivity.

The First World War also played its part in changing the status and roles of women. Many women took on roles and responsibilities previously undertaken by men; they became the head of the household and breadwinners. Women worked in factories and drove ambulances; some became nurses. This shift in roles had a radical impact on women and brought about the onset of early feminism and established the Suffragette Movement.

The railway was hugely influential in transforming existence; it enabled the growth of cities and transformed landscapes by blurring the division between urban and rural. There was an increase in mobility and communications, and the creation of the railway's own time led to an eradication of old notions of time and space. In 1911, the Greenwich Mean Time was adopted as the universal standard. At the turn of the century, the telephone, invented by Alexander Graham Bell, became widely available, enabling almost instant communication throughout the world, which completely altered perceptions of time and space.

In the late nineteenth century, the first cars were produced, and by 1908, with the introduction of the Model-T by Henry Ford, mass production arrived. The development of cars cut the time it took to transport people, information and goods from one place to another, which too had implications for time and space, communication and the individual's vision of themselves, and the world.

As a result of evolutions in technology, new forms of entertainment came into operation; these included the wireless, gramophone and cinema. The cinematograph was created by the Lumiere brothers and was first demonstrated in Paris in 1895; this was then quickly followed, a year later, by a showing in London. The moving picture gave the opportunity to reach wide audiences, linking people across time and space and synchronizing society. The first films, shown in music halls and at fair grounds and circuses, were short, only a few minutes long and portrayed music hall acts or sporting events. However, advances in film technology soon made it possible to extend the running time and longer narratives screened in cinemas became popular. By the end of the First World War, a film industry was established in most industrialized countries.

Photography began to assume the status of fine art and questioned traditional modes of representation. The photographer Alfred Stieglitz opened a salon in New York and showed the latest European works by Picasso and other friends of Gertrude Stein. Commercial printing technology made photography popular.

In Europe and America, there was an emergence of mass print media so that it became cheaper to print exact copies of manuscript rather than to alter one by hand. Edison had invented the phonograph, which led to a wave of magazines, newspapers, printed sheet music and children's books being produced and read, following a steady increase in literacy since the 1870 Education Act. The term 'bestseller' was used in the 1890s; these novels appealed to a mass readership, who sought entertainment as opposed to intellectual stimulation. Subsequently, bestsellers were published in journals.

There were also developments in science which further altered and shaped worldviews. In 1905, for example, there was the publication of Albert Einstein's *Special Theory of Relativity*, which challenged Newton's model. Einstein's theory argued that the speed of light was absolute, and the two absolutes of the Newtonian model, space and time, therefore, could not be. And Max Planck's quantum theory denied a complete understanding of reality, which, in turn, had an impact on worldviews.

These changes in science led to an interest in human life beyond that of science, to include psychology. Sigmund Freud's *The Interpretation of Dreams* brought about a fascination with the unconscious mind, and in 1859, Darwin's *Origin of Species* threatened to undermine the Bible's legitimacy to explain the unexplainable. And so, during this period, there were shifts in values and beliefs, in particular those surrounding the bourgeois family, morality, the new woman and homosexual, all of which will be explored in this section of the book.

However, it is now important to move from discussing historical events, innovations, values and beliefs to looking at modernist cultural expression and the implications this had for some fiction writers who sought to experiment with their creative practice.

What was modernism?

Modernism can be seen as a response to the condition of modernity, a transformation that swept through the arts in response to the huge developments in technology, science and psychology and the social and ideological changes in beliefs, systems, ways of life and attitudes to class structures and values – the new mapping of landscapes and frontiers.

Modernism questioned much of the form of pre-twentieth-century artistic practice and was viewed as an attempt to break with realism; it represented 'a paradigm shift both in the history of literature, and in the way literary history has been constructed' (Pykett, 1995, p. 10). In addition, it has been described as a 'cultural temper pervading all the arts', one which was 'opaque, unfamiliar, deliberately disturbing, experiment in form' (Turner, 1990, p. 19). The ideas that came out of modernism were progressive and pushed back boundaries, and the artistic works created during this movement were concerned with a knowledge of the past, but were also imbued with a sense of *the future has not happened yet*. One of modernism's most ' ... distinguishing features is the way it crossed many conventional boundaries, including boundaries of nation, but also of discipline' (Wilson, pp. 3–4). However, for the purposes of this book, it is appropriate to illustrate how modernism impacted upon fiction.

How did modernism impact upon fiction?

Artistic evolution is not simply an aesthetic event arising from nowhere; it arises from social and ideological change as has already been established. The historical, scientific and technological shifts that took place, in particular during the first half of the twentieth century, especially those affecting transport, culture and communication, resulted in an upheaval in culture, one that overturned many previous aesthetic tenets and principles of art works, including those of fiction.

Modernism impacted upon fiction in new and exciting ways. Literary works created during this time attempted to capture this unsettling and yet highly exciting period of history; it brought a fresh consciousness to creative practice, with writers rejecting previous literary conventions in order to explore new techniques and strategies.

Modernism's impact led to an increase in experimentation by writers, which, in turn, resulted in many new literary techniques and forms evolving to express the complexity and chaos brought about by the acceleration of change. For some writers, the shifting and turbulent society was an incentive for them to turn their focus inwards – rather than to focus outwards – on a world where the individual's place was uncertain and confused.

In modern fiction, there was a move away from the traditional realist novel. Literary works were no longer so concerned with linear plot; they were most interested in the fragmentation of form. There was also a preoccupation with the relativity of time which led to a disruption to linear flow, a breaking down of beginning, middle and end. In 1926, Thomas Hardy remarked, somewhat concerned, that everything had changed; there used to be a beginning, middle and an end, but this form had ceased to exist. Indeed, there were experiments in narrative sequencing, generating consciously confused narratives which moved backwards and forwards in time; this experimentation brought about the rejection of pinning excitement on linear plot, and it also led to a decline in the use of dramatic tension, suspense and closed endings. For example, Marcel Proust's *In Search of Lost Time* is a novel which explores memory and is in constant flux; it moves backwards and forwards in time, moments of the past and the present having equal reality.

Fiction became self-reflexive, that is, the work was not a representation of reality as realist art was, but a representation of the processes of representation: a work that explored its own structure. So the way the story was told became as important as the story itself. For example, in Ernest Hemingway's *A Farewell to Arms*, Hemingway treats narrative and dialogue as self-conscious exercises by which the author himself recognizes to be exercises. As Leigh Wilson writes:

> One of the things which distinguishes what we now call modernism from many previous kinds of writing was the extent to which the literary and the critical were intertwined. Modernist writers were highly conscious of critical questions surrounding their writing, questions of how they wrote and what writing was for, and the links between themselves and other innovative writers. (p. 125)

This led to a rethinking of the relationship between fiction and reality, an exploration of how one saw the world rather than what one actually saw. This was confusing to some readers who were unaccustomed to plotless novels, readers who were more familiar with literature that entertained and told stories as a means of escape from the harshness of reality. Instead, fiction posed questions; for example, what constituted reality? How could the world be perceived?

Trying to discover *new* ways of describing character and human experience fascinated the modern writer, now that human existence had changed and the essence of human nature was being debated. So, writers experimented with new techniques within their fiction in an attempt to explore and grapple with a world that they could no longer understand. And now that fiction was no longer focused on narrative interest, writers became absorbed with the psychological mood of characters, also, atmospheres, epiphanies and the blurring of the boundaries between fact and fiction. Modernist writers were keen to communicate the inner experience and thoughts of their characters as they occurred rather than their exterior worlds. Virginia Woolf illustrated one of the most endorsed priorities of modern fiction when she wrote:

> Look within and life, it seems, is very far from being 'like this'. Examine for a moment an ordinary mind on an ordinary day. The mind receives a myriad impressions – trivial, fantastic, evanescent, or engraved with the sharpness of steel. From all sides they come, an incessant shower of innumerable atoms; and as they fall, as they shape themselves into the life of Monday or Tuesday, the accent falls differently from of old … Life is not a series of gig-lamps symmetrically arranged; life is a luminous halo, a semi-transparent envelope surrounding us from the beginning of consciousness to the end. Is it not the task of the novelist to convey this varying, this unknown and uncircumscribed spirit, whatever aberration or complexity it may display, with as little mixture of the alien and external as possible? We are not pleading merely for courage and sincerity; we are suggesting that the proper stuff of fiction is a little other than custom would have us believe it. (Woolf, 'Modern Fiction', Collected Essays (note 1), p. 107)

And so, new forms and writing techniques came into being, for example, symbols, motifs, fragmentation, dislocation, juxtaposition, collage, ambiguity, montage, stream of consciousness and multiple narratives, as the focus came to be on a character's conscious and subconscious mind, as opposed to character development and plot. D. H. Lawrence employed numerous symbols in his work. In *Sons and Lovers*, the swing became a symbol of the love–hate relationship between Paul and Miriam and the ash tree a symbol for the dark, mysterious forces of nature. William Faulkner also used symbols in *The Sound and the Fury*. Quentin's watch conveyed a character trapped by time, unable to move beyond his memories of the past, whereas his brother Jason had no use for the past, focusing on the present. So, the text experimented with form; there were frequent time shifts. Also present are a stream of consciousness, unconventional punctuation and sentence construction, multiple points of view and multiple voices, which reflected a world invaded by the disembodied voice of technology, in particular the radio.

The way language was used was another way modernism impacted upon literary works. In modernist fiction language was used not simply to convey a message or to tell a story, but to be an artistic tool in its own right; it became musical, lyrical, multilingual and was used in *new* imaginative and inventive ways. James Joyce in *Finnegans Wake* used 'riverrun', two words together which suggested a constantly flowing river of meaning, one which invited the reader to become an interpreter of meaning. James Joyce and also Gertrude Stein experimented with syntax, so that narratives had richness, complexity and an ambiguity of form, and content, which provoked readers to look at writing, and the world around them, with fresh eyes.

What is the impact of modernist texts on contemporary texts?

It can be seen that modernism impacted dramatically upon modernist fiction, *new* literature emerged, a literature that was complex and difficult, one that was concerned with innovation and experimentation, a literature brought about by a need to understand, and to reflect, the shifting times. However, the impact of modernist fiction has left its legacy and there are currently a number of contemporary writers who are using modernist techniques within their fiction.

In *The Hours*, American writer Michael Cunningham takes Woolf's life and works as a source of inspiration. Each section of the book imitates Mrs Dalloway by being restricted to the events of a single day and embraces the technique of stream of consciousness and switching between consciousnesses.

The Australian novelist and academic Gail Jones's novel *Five Bells* has its roots in the modernist tradition, in the work of James Joyce, but more explicitly in the work of Virginia Woolf. *Five Bells*, like *The Hours*, is reminiscent of Mrs Dalloway; the narrative traces intersecting lives across a city during the course of a single day. As in Woolf's fiction, however, the moments of coincidence in the physical world are not as important as the subtle connections that lie beneath the surface. Pei Xing and Catherine are linked by recurrent images of snow. For Pei Xing, there is the memory of snowfall in her childhood, as well as the recollection of snow in *Doctor Zhivago*. Catherine's thoughts of snow remind her of James Joyce's 'The Dead' and also of her partner's passion for Russian novels, in particular *Doctor Zhivago*.

British author Jon Mcgregor's *If Nobody Speaks of Remarkable Things* is a novel which moves away from pinning all excitement on plot or dramatic tension; it charts the effects of a single incident and is written in a prose which is as precise, concise and evocative as poetry.

Another British writer who employs modernist techniques is Amy Sackville; her novel *Still Point* also takes place on a single summer day. She is not so much concerned with plot in this novel as exploring a twenty-first-century marriage juxtaposed against an account of a polar exhibition. It is the use of language that is so striking about this text and her more recent text *Orkney*. The language is as sumptuous and rich as poetry, with luminous descriptions of the landscapes. It is no surprise to discover that Amy Sackville specialized in modernism at Exeter College, Oxford.

Umbrella by British writer Will Self is a novel based on Oliver Sack's *Awakening*, a non-fiction account of treating patients with encephalitis lethargica (EL) in the late 1960s. *Umbrella* shares modernism's preoccupation with time and memory and employs many modern techniques. That is, it is a non-linear text which moves backwards and forwards in time; it has three time frames and four points of view. Self employs stream of consciousness, reminiscent of Woolf and Joyce; there are few paragraph breaks and no chapters. Indeed, the title and epigraph have been lifted from James Joyce's *Ulysses*: 'A brother is as easily forgotten as an umbrella.' Within this text, Self plays with language; it is like listening to a wireless as voices fade in and out and mix, allowing Self to make connections between the mind, war and technology. Audrey Death has been in a state of semi-consciousness for half a century in Friern Barnet Mental Hospital after contracting EL; then, in 1971 the psychiatrist Dr Zack Busner arrives. He attempts to bring her back to life with a new drug. The novel revolves around Audrey Death's experiences of Edwardian London, her work in a munitions factory during the First World War, her socialist lover and her involvement with the suffragettes, interwoven with her two brothers fighting in the Second World War.

And so, it can be seen that the legacy of modernism lives on in the works of contemporary writers. It is now important to investigate in the following chapters of this book what modernist writers were doing in their texts and how they were doing it, so that all readers and writers of experimental fiction can use these techniques within their own creative writing practice.

Form and Fiction

In order to enable readers and writers of experimental fiction to deconstruct modernist texts, to understand what these works are doing and to read them with a writer's eye, this chapter will investigate the relationship between the trauma of the First World War and a moving-away from traditional linear plot. In addition, it will explore the experimentation with form, illustrating how fiction became more abstract, dislocated and fragmented and how it experimented with writing techniques to reflect its themes.

What was the form of fiction prior to modernity?

Prior to the First Wold War, Victorian fiction tended to be linear in its form: beginning, middle and ending to reflect a realistic secure world vision. Fiction explored moral, emotional or other problems, which disturbed the lives of its characters. However, they almost always resolved these problems so that order was restored and to a great extent the characters' equilibrium recovered, for example, *Great Expectations* by Charles Dickens, in which the protagonist, Pip, longed to be a gentleman. He received a large sum of money from an anonymous benefactor and consequently moved to London, leaving behind his family, Joe and Biddy, whom he was ashamed of because they were poor. His wealth had changed him, not for the better; however, at the end of the book, he matured as a result of his experiences and became reunited with his family.

What was the form of modern fiction?

The First World War (1914–18) was a global war; it led to the death of millions of people across the world as the result of technological developments. Therefore, the world vision shifted to illustrate a world collapsing in fragments as a result of the chaos and dislocation brought about by the war. Fiction mirrored this shift in vision. Consequently, rigid constraints of form were discarded, fiction too became fragmented and there was an abandonment of the traditional linear plot. Fragmentation was also used to portray the sense of dislocation soldiers experienced as a result of their time spent in the trenches seeing their comrades being shot, lying wounded or dying and to capture the shell shock and sense of alienation soldiers' families experienced. After the war, almost everyone would have suffered loss and bereavement.

Experiment with this: Learning to Experiment with Fragmentation

Write the opening of a short story
It is the First World War. You are writing from the point of view of a soldier in the trenches. You have been shot. Allow the mind to freeze to capture the shock, then your mind kick-starts and wanders. Write without censoring to capture your fragmented thoughts and impressions, sensations and feelings. Record what you feel, see, hear, touch, taste and smell. Allow the writing to be fragmented and erratic to capture this traumatic experience.

What was the structure of some modernist fiction?

Following the First World War, a previous way of life was demolished forever. In addition to the sense of alienation and dislocation that imbued much of the world, there were, however, advancements in medicine, technology and science and developments in psychology, philosophy, education and the roles and status of women, which led to new ways of thinking about the world and human beings. Consequently writers experimented within their fiction in order to present the structure, connections and *new* experiences of life in a different way.

Some modernist fiction portrayed the war as an event that cut through time and history as societies and people's lives were divided as before, during and after the war. *To the Lighthouse* by Virginia Woolf illustrates this division: there is a holiday, followed by a destruction of lives and then a sense of looking back. In *Jacob's Room*, Woolf also displays a fiction presented in fragments. The book follows the life of Jacob: his childhood in Scarborough, his education in Oxford, his life in London, a trip to Greece and it ends after his death.

Experiment with this: Learning to Experiment with the Structure of Fiction

Write a short story in which a young man's life is divided into the following slices: a happy childhood, an exciting first love affair, his traumatic experiences in the First World War, his homecoming and, finally, his struggle to adapt to life after the war.

What writing techniques did modern writers use to reflect the themes of modern fiction?

During the modernist period, fiction became a space in which complex forms of collective and individual trauma could be played out. Many writers engaged with and responded to the war; for example, D. H. Lawrence, author of the provocative *Lady Chatterley's Lover*, wrote of the bruise of the war. Likewise, the world before and after the First World War became a major theme of Virginia Woolf's work, that is, the idea of how to make sense of the changes brought about by the war specifically from the point of view of a woman who had not actually seen battle but had felt its impact is central to *Mrs Dalloway*. *To the Lighthouse* is suffused with the melancholy and mourning of war and *Jacob's Room*'s atmosphere is oppressive with the foreboding of Jacob's coming death, his ultimate death during the war and the questions raised by it. Loss of life and technological innovation for destructive purposes – machine guns, tanks aircraft, shells, chemical weapons – resulted in devastating consequences and brought into question the very concept of civilization. In turn, this question provided a theme for modern fiction and resulted in writers producing work that experimented with a variety of writing techniques, such as multiple voices, multiple points of view and multiple narratives to depict the themes of trauma, confusion, angst and the questions the war incited.

Experiment with this: Learning to Write with Multiple Voices and Multiple Points of View to Reflect the Theme of Trauma

Write a scene from a novel

Imagine a soldier in the First World War who is homesick and is thinking about life at home. Write an interior monologue of his thoughts, feelings and impressions. He is hearing 'other' voices too, 'other' perspectives, those of his mother, father and sweetheart; include these in the monologue to create a multi-layered text which switches backwards and forwards in time.

Worldview and Fiction

This chapter shows contemporary writers of experimental fiction how modernist writing practice provides a more authentic depiction of thought processes and how the world is experienced, and perceived, now as opposed to the nineteenth-century realist fiction worldview, so that they too can experiment with a variety of writing techniques to explore how we *see* the world rather than what we actually *see*.

What were the priorities for modernist fiction?

Modernist writers were very much concerned with exploring the workings of the human consciousness. The phrase 'stream of consciousness' was first coined by an American psychologist William James in 1890 in his work *Principles of Psychology* and it was William's brother, Henry James, who introduced this term into fiction.

Stream of consciousness is a literary style that mingles memories, feelings, impressions and thoughts in an illogical order with a disregard for the conventional use of syntax, grammar and punctuation. Many modernist writers experimented with this style within their fiction, for example, Dorothy Richardson in her work *Pilgrimage* and William Faulkner in *The Sound and Fury* (1929). James Joyce's *Ulysses* (1922) is also an example of a novel whose events are the workings of the human consciousness.

Taking her lead from Dorothy Richardson, Virginia Woolf continually experimented in her fiction, searching for a new form for the novel, one that would capture and follow the 'flight of the mind', the mind's interior and the flow of consciousness unfolding in time. This new form prioritized shifts in perspective, as well as being concerned with thoughts and feelings. For example, one minute a character's thoughts would be consumed with studying decoration on upholstery, and in the next minute, examining human nature.

Modernist writers considered that the Victorian novelists treated their minds as something static, whereas by looking into their own minds, they discovered that consciousness was erratic, not static at all. Consciousness was ever flowing, shattering into a myriad of sensations and impressions, so that one was at the whim of one's thoughts and feelings – thoughts and feelings that were difficult to control. However, Woolf came to the conclusion that thoughts are ultimately held together by the self, *a* self that emerges from these fleeting impressions and interpretations of the world – through the stories one tells one's self about the world, and one's experiences in it.

In order to arrive at her discoveries, Woolf explored her ideas through her fiction; she experimented with form and writing techniques: fragmentation, stream of consciousness and multiple perspectives. Septimus Smith, a character in *Mrs Dalloway*, is a shell-shocked poet and a veteran of the First World War. He conveys to the reader this wandering of consciousness; his mind divides into multiple, contradicting thoughts and feelings, at any given moment, in time. However, with the writing of *To the Lighthouse*, Woolf 'provided a kind of paradigm for the new priorities of modernist fiction, for its growing inclination to turn from the world to the mind' (Stevenson, p. 61).

Why did the modernist writers experiment with anti-linear fiction?

Modernist work departed from linear chronology to show how anti-linear thought processes more accurately convey how the world is perceived. This idea of 'quick-silverness' of mind, as referred to by Woolf, is a key concept to the understanding of modernist fiction.

> ## Experiment with this: Learning to Experiment with 'Quick-Silverness' of Mind
>
> Write a scene from a novel. Create a character at an early twentieth-century dinner party. Go into the character's mind. Do not write a description of the events and other characters in the room, but write the random impressions and feelings, the diverse and conflicting thoughts your character has about the other guests and the dining experience, as they flow incessantly in the character's mind.

How was reality perceived in modern fiction?

Modernist writers were seeking to address the complex realities around them; this was at odds with the way reality had previously been perceived. Modernist writers were endeavouring to describe reality as it was *actually* experienced. To do this, as already stated, it was essential that the form of the novel had to be transformed. At the end of *A Room of One's Own*, Woolf asks: 'What is meant by "reality"'? For Woolf it seems that art 'is an extension of reality' (Woolf, A Critical Memoir, Winifred Holtby (1936) (A new preface, Marion Shaw, 2007), Continuum, p. 41). It is

> something very erratic, very undependable-now to be found in a dusty road, now in a scrap of newspaper in the street, now in a daffodil in the sun ... But whatever it touches, it fixes and makes permanent. That is what remains over when the skin of the day has been cast in the hedge; that is what is left of the past time and of our loves and hates. Now the writer, as I think, has the chance to live more than other people in the presence of this reality. It is his business to find it and collect it and communicate it to the rest of us.

In other words, reality is constructed in the mind; it is about *how* the world is seen by the observer rather than what is *actually* seen.

Experiment with this: Learning to Write *How* We See the World Rather than What We *Actually* See

A character in a novel is making a journey by train for the first time. Consider how they feel about this new experience. What kind of person is your character: optimistic, pessimistic? Are they nervous, excited, happy, fearful? How will this affect the way they see the world around them? Will they fixate on the size, speed, noise of the train? Will they be exhilarated, terrified, intrigued? Now write the journey. Bear in mind, this is not necessarily about how the world/train/journey actually *is*, but how it *appears* to your character.

How did modernist writers react against realism?

Woolf saw each artist's vision of reality as being individual. This had implications in terms of plurality and fluidity of perception, something also being investigated by philosophers and psychologists of the era. This led James Joyce in *Ulysses* (1922) to abandon any coherent voice, so that the work had a dislocation similar to that of a dream. The modernist considered that life is not realism. And so, many traditional realistic techniques, such as description, plots of external action, dramatic scenes, climaxes and resolutions, were abandoned. Writers went into themselves. Joyce, Woolf, Richardson and Faulkner reacted against realism through streams of consciousness; new forms of prose emerged, prose that was closely allied to poetry.

According to Woolf:

> Poets present sensations, emotions and processes of thought, with only lightly indicated backgrounds. They reveal, rather than explain. They suggest. They illuminate. They flash a torch through the darkness on to a child's green bucket, an aster trembling violently in the wind… Poets have an immense advantage over novelists. (Memoir, pp. 101–2)

Woolf wanted to write prose but she also wanted to have the freedom of the poet. The poet is able to experience intense perception, for example, how the cold feet of insects must feel upon the bark of a tree, in *The Mark on the Wall*.

And so she was continually experimenting:

> ...stretching her prose to the fullest limits of intelligibility, and sometimes beyond, seeing how far it was possible to discard description, discard narrative, discard the link – sentences which bind ideas together, seeing how far it was possible to write her prose from within, like poetry, giving it a life of its own. She was devising her new techniques; she was testing possibilities...she had begun to question the necessity of all the heavy impedimenta of plot, narrative... (Holtby, pp. 99–100)

Experiment with this: Learning How to Write Prose Like a Poet

Using the title 'A Child's Green Bucket', write a short story in which you privilege sensations, perceptions and emotions over plot. Experiment with revealing rather than explaining, suggesting rather than saying, illuminating rather than stating. Write prose with the freedom of a poet.

How did the modernist writers *see* the world?

Modernist writers saw the world through multiple perspectives, both micro and macro. The weaving of past and present, like moving from image to image, was attributed, in part, to the techniques of the cinema. Perspectives

> ...suddenly diminish to the consciousness of a snail, who sees cliffs and lakes and round boulders of grey stone...then suddenly they swing to the vast bird's-eye view from an aeroplane flying above the trees. (Woolf, pp. 110–1)

Experiment with this: Learning to Use Multiple Perspectives

Imagine you are seeing the world through the lens of a camera. Write a scene from a novel in which the lens captures a bird's eye view of the landscape below, then suddenly zones in on specific features: a church, a stained glass window in the church, a spider's web spun in the corner of the window, a fly trapped in the web struggling to break free; then swing back into the sky, to a bird, a cloud, a drop of rain, a rainbow – write from all of these perspectives.

Gender Crisis

This chapter explores the impact the *New Woman* and the *Homosexual* or *Decadent* had on the content, form and writing techniques of modernist fiction, so that readers and writers of contemporary experimental fiction can comprehend what the modernist texts are doing and incorporate these strategies into their own fiction.

Who illustrated the crisis of gender definition and representation?

The most dramatic examples at the turn of the century which best illustrated the crisis of gender definition and representation were the *New Woman* and the *Homosexual* or *Decadent*. What is interesting about the movement into modernism of these figures is that they anticipated so many of the later concerns of postmodern writers, in terms of both form and ideas about insecure and unsettled identities, as they challenged gender and social boundaries. This resulted in such questions being asked as: what does it mean to be a man or a woman? Are men and women simply biological states of being or are they constructs imposed by society? To investigate such questions, new writing techniques evolved; as already discussed, the writer turned their attention inwards, rather outwards, at the exterior world. The stream of consciousness was a technique writers used to explore the inner world.

What role did women have in the making of modernism?

Lyn Pykett suggests that women had an important role to play 'in the making of modernism' (Pykett, 1995, p. 2). In the early years of the twentieth century, there was both a social crisis, how women lived their lives, and a crisis in representation. The struggles included both political and cultural representation. During this period, the women's movement was seeking to improve women's social and political positions and

> Modern woman (hence modern man), modern marriage, free love, the artistic aspirations of women, female eroticism ... It was precisely these issues, and indeed, the whole context of the late Victorian dissolution with which self-consciously modern novelists engaged – from H. G. Wells, E. M. Forster, and D. H. Lawrence to May Sinclair, Virginia Woolf, Dorothy Richardson and Rebecca West. (Pykett, 1995, p. 15)

By the beginning of the twentieth century, most men of 21 years and over had the right to vote in general elections. However, all women were excluded. Therefore, this period saw the 'votes for women' campaign with the founding of the *Women's Social and Political Union* in 1903, led by Emmeline Pankhurst. Suffragette militancy, which included hunger strikes, stone throwing, setting fire to empty houses and cutting telegraph wires, challenged the notion of femininity and masculinity and initiated a break of traditional behaviour between men and women. In 1911, Dora Marsden founded *The Freewoman*, a paper that linked challenges to conventional sexuality with feminism; it also sought to open debates on wages for motherhood. Later, Ezra Pound persuaded Marsden to include literary material and the paper became a space for experimental writing, including that of James Joyce and T. S. Eliot.

So, it can be seen that the period of modernity saw the rise of the first wave of feminism, which consolidated in the women's suffrage movement, during the fight for the vote. Clearly, the aims of the suffrage were to enable women to find their own voice and assert an identity not imposed upon them by patriarchy.

Woolf paid tribute to the women fighting for the vote through the character Mary Datchet, the suffrage worker, in *Night and Day*. Although Woolf chose to adhere to her desire to be an artist, as opposed to sacrificing this desire to enfranchising the woman citizen, at a time when many women writers, artists, actresses and musicians were very much torn between their obligations to their practice and their obligations to society. The dilemma of these creative practitioners was: how could they create when there was not a single woman with a vote, when women worked, cooked, cleaned and bore children?

Experiment with this: Learning to Use Stream of Consciousness

Write a passage from a novel in which a female writer is wrestling with her dilemma: should she simply be a writer and create? Or, should she fight for the right to vote along with her comrades? Use stream of consciousness to capture her outpouring of thoughts and inner conflict, that is, write without stopping for ten minutes. Do not be concerned with punctuation and syntax. Simply be present and go with the flow of writing. Do not censor the writer's concerns and questions that she has in her mind.

In February 1922, *Life* magazine had a cover on which it displayed a young woman known as *a flapper*. A *flapper*, who exemplified the new social and political freedoms available to some women following the First World War, was a hedonistic, often promiscuous, single woman, who enjoyed wearing make-up and fashionable clothes, and whose pastimes included smoking, drinking, sniffing cocaine and dancing to jazz music, this being the era of dance crazes, which emerged from the African American districts in the United Sates, in particular in New Orleans.

Flappers liked to cause a *flap* purely for the fun of it and enjoyed being seen in a culture of seeing. They challenged previous representations of women and abandoned corsets. In addition, they wore short skirts, had their hair cut in bobs, often had boyish figures which implied androgyny and had a distinct slang vocabulary, for example, 'sugar' meaning 'money', 'feather' meaning 'small talk', 'slat' meaning 'young man', 'half-cut' meaning 'intoxicated'.

Young women who were considered to be flappers included the dancer Josephine Baker, who danced exotically in a skirt consisting of fake bananas; Zelda Fitzgerald, the wife of Scott Fitzgerald, both of whom spent the summer of 1924 in Montmartre celebrating the success of *The Great Gatsby*; Tamara de Lempicka, who was a painter; Nancy Cunard an avant-garde poet; and Diana Cooper, who went on stage and was said to be D. H. Lawrence's Lady Artemis in his novel *Aaron's Rod* (1922).

Experiment with this: Learning to Experiment with Language and Representations of Women

Research the language, clothes, hairstyles and lifestyles of flappers. Write a scene from a novel in which a group of flappers have fun at a dance hall.

Who challenged the sexual conventions of previous generations?

Sigmund Freud's work and ideas challenged conventions in matters of sexuality and sexual identity. Freud regarded individuals as being motivated largely by sexual desires, desires that were often repressed. The reshaping of sexuality was explored in the work of such writers as James Joyce and D. H. Lawrence, work which initiated the change of attitudes towards obscenity and censorship, leading to an increased openness. In *Women in Love*, through the relationship of Gerald Crich and Rupert Birkin, Lawrence explores themes of homosexuality, in particular in a famous erotically charged scene in the novel in which the two men wrestle naked.

The *Bloomsbury Group* played their part in challenging the conventions and morals of previous generations. The group included

Virginia Woolf, Leonard Woolf, Vanessa Bell, Roger Fry and Clive Bell, to name a few. The *Bloomsbury Group* was interested in new artistic practices, ideas and sexual representations in fiction. They championed personal freedom, including the right to experiment sexually, which also included homosexual practice.

Homosexuality was illegal in Britain until 1967. However, in addition to D. H. Lawrence, writers such as Gertrude Stein, Ronald Firbank, Djuna Barnes, Radclyffe Hall, Vita Sackville-West and Sylvia Townsend Warner wrote about homosexual practice with candour. Maybe this was partly due to the trials surrounding Oscar Wilde's homosexuality in 1895. He claimed that art is not moral, and therefore, the aim of the author is not a moralistic one. Ultimately, Wilde's imprisonment challenged assumptions about 'normal' relationships.

How did the modernists reflect upon the experience of gender?

The Modernists reflected on the experience of gender, researching into the psychological experiences that defined each individual which led them to critique the ideas of masculinity and femininity, not simply in terms of legal representation, but in terms of the aesthetic. Virginia Woolf was concerned with whether women writers should simply replicate a male perspective or if it was possible to produce a feminine aesthetic. To do so, it was necessary for the modernists to look deep inside character, paying full attention to consciousness and the nature of being. It led to a number of questions being asked: Do men and women view the world differently? Do men and women use the same language in their speaking and writing? And so, modernists broke from the fixed gender mores of Victorian society and explored sexuality with a new frankness. Therefore, in the early twentieth century, there was a new spirit of sexual liberation, a spirit alluded to by Virginia Nicholson as experiments in living; this, in part, was due to a rising bohemian culture, a culture in which open discussions of sexual matters sometimes led to open relationships, particularly true of the *Bloomsbury Group*. Fiction explored a freer sexuality for men and women and this changed the representations of both sexes in fiction, for example, Grant Allen's, *The Woman Who Did* (1895), H. G. Wells's *Ann Veronica* (1909) and Virginia Woolf's *Orlando* (1928).

Experiment with this: Learning to Experiment with Switching Gender Roles and Multiple Narratives

Write a short story in which in the first part of the narrative the character is a man. However, this character goes to sleep and wakes to discover that he has metamorphosed into a woman overnight: the same person, the same personality, but a woman's body. Now tell *her* narrative. Explore the magnitude of becoming a woman; that is, is the restricting clothes she has to wear, for example, a corset? Also, show in the narrative the impact her body has on men; for example, in *Orlando*, there is an incident in which a flash of an ankle nearly results in a sailor falling to his death.

The City and Fiction

This chapter illustrates how modernist writers found the city a source of inspiration for creativity and how it became the setting for a number of modernist texts, for example, James Joyce's *Ulysses* and Joseph Conrad's *The Secret Agent*. It shows how the changing face of the city, with its dizzying array of *new* experiences, transformed modern fiction with the intention of enabling contemporary readers and writers to understand the texts and the modernist era, so that they could enrich their own fiction, by experimenting with modernist techniques.

What led to the rise of modern cities?

Modern industry and the growth of the railways led to a wave of urbanization and the rise of great cities. Indeed, modernism can be seen as a response to the shock of the *new* of city, a city which embodies the spirit and time of modernity and was perceived as a symbol of capitalism. Major modernist cities included Paris, Berlin, New York, Vienna, St. Petersburg and Vienna.

Why was the modern city an exciting place?

For a number of reasons, many modernist writers found the rapidly changing modern city an exciting and dynamic place to be. The city provided a stimulating environment, one which had a multiplicity of voices and a variety of experiences. These experiences included walking in crowds of people, observing the rapid development of technology, admiring the architecture and gazing upon the goods being sold in department stores and arcades. There were art works to view and museums to explore.

Developments in transport were exciting experiences to be had in the city; for example, the Metro in Paris was built in 1900 by the engineer Fulgence Bienvenue. The first line ferried passengers from the Port Maillot to Vincennes in the unbelievable time of twenty minutes; previously it took an hour and a half by carriage. And so, the pace of life became much quicker and the experience of cities much richer.

There was a bombardment of sensual experiences, which led to a heightened sense of awareness and consciousness. The *Paris Exposition* of 1900 involved a number of simulations: an exotic Indian landscape with stuffed animals, treasures and merchandise; an exhibit representing Spain at the time of the Moors with interiors and courtyards; a Trans-Siberian panorama which placed spectators in a real railway car which moved along a track, while canvas was unrolled outside the window to give an impression of Siberia. Experience offered by carnivals and fairs in Paris, especially after the 1848 revolution, was bizarre: animals became humans, humans became animals. There were the new department stores and arcades showing consumer items, associated with exotica and romance.

The flaneur Charles Baudelaire enjoyed walking through the streets, milling among the crowds, absorbing all the experiences and gazing upon the capitalist world. A flaneur is a representative of modernity and a personification of the urban, illustrating many different relationships with the city; a flaneur observes and yet is part of the city. He experiences the city as a place of meetings, a place of flux and collisions, a place of ordered chaos, in which he can experience fleeting impressions and enjoy the spectacle of the city.

The city was a space in which to examine modernist concerns, for example, representation of time and space. In 1884, the *Prime Meridian Conference* established Greenwich as the zero meridian and the exact length of the day was determined. In 1912, the *International Conference on Time* was held in Paris; it established a worldwide time system centred on Greenwich. However, the modernists considered the true experience of time was to be found by looking within, at one's memories and impressions, thoughts and feelings.

Experiment with this: Learning to Look Within and Record Impressions, Thoughts and Feelings of the Modern City

Create a character, a flaneur, who is walking the city streets of your choice. Enter this flaneur's mind and record their thoughts, feelings and impressions as they experience the city. What is the city like? How has it changed? What do they see, hear, touch, taste, smell? How do they experience time and space? Are any memories evoked by their experiences?

What was cafe and nightclub culture?

The city became a place where writers could simply absorb the atmosphere and meet with other writers to discuss their work, and so cafe nightclub culture ensued. In 1922, a new nightclub opened in Paris: *Le Boeuf sur le Toit*; its proprietor was a man called Louis Moyses, who named the club after a popular musical written by Jean Cocteau; he was a man who 'set the tone of Parisian modernity and embodied its heady, stylish spirit' (Jackson, p. 30). Jean Cocteau, influenced by Oscar Wilde, published a collection of poems in 1909. However, inspired by Diaghilev and the Ballet Russes, he turned his attention to stage design. *Le Boeuf*, as it became known, was the place to be seen and the meeting place for all the famous business people, publishers and artists of the day, a place where they could flirt, show off their designer clothes, dance, drink American-style cocktails and, most importantly, discuss ideas and artistic works. 'The club inspired at least two books about the period – *Au Temps du Boeuf sur le Toit* by Maurice Sachs, and *Quand le Boeuf* by Jacques – and was mentioned in countless others' (Jackson, p. 33).

Experiment with this: Learning to Become Familiar with Modernist Writing Techniques

Write a scene from a novel which is set in *Le Boeuf*. In this scene two writers, real or imagined, discuss their latest literary work and the writing techniques they are experimenting with. The two writers are approached by a publisher. Write the conversation that ensues between the writers and the publisher. Capture the atmosphere of the nightclub.

Which modern writers explored the city in their literary works?

However, as a result of the rapidly changing city, which was altering perceptions, as well as excitement, there came a sense of isolation and loneliness. These became reoccurring themes in fiction, which used a fragmented, non-linear form to suggest this dislocation and the shifting vision of what it was to be a human being.

Many writers used the city as a source of inspiration and a setting for their fiction, often providing the backdrop for their fiction, for example, James Joyce used Dublin in *Ulysses* and the *Dubliners*. Joseph Conrad employed London in *The Secret Agent*. Likewise, Virginia Woolf's *Mrs Dalloway* and *The Waves* exude a sense of unreality, attributed to the facelessness and depersonalizing of the crowd, and the corruption of the city, London, and yet, there is also the fascinating quality of the city. As Clariss Dolloway in *Mrs Dolloway* is walking through London, her mind is a veritable city of thoughts. The idea of solitary lives makes its way into the core of the stories of James Joyce; the isolation of individual consciousness, that there is no escape from the self or from the dilapidated dark city streets, forms the subject of the *Dubliners*.

Langston Hughes depicted the lives of African Americans living in Harlem, New York, blossoming into the Harlem Renaissance, what

American poet, novelist, social activist and playwright Langston called his reason for writing. Embodying the new literary form, jazz poetry, he wrote about the period 'the negro was in vogue', when night clubs, featuring jazz, flourished. Despite material wealth, young Americans of the 1920s were the 'lost generation', so named by Gertrude Stein. Hemingway's *The Sun Also Rises* (1926) and Fitzgerald's *This Side of Paradise* (1920) evoke the disillusionment of the 'lost generation'. Hughes' first novel was *Not Without Laughter* (1930).

What new styles of writing did the city inspire?

City life inspired new styles and forms of writing in an attempt to capture the modern world. There were public and private spaces which led to writers exploring the inner world and outer reality using techniques such as stream of consciousness and interior monologue. And so, with city life being ever challenging, it is to the inner world that characters in modernist fiction retreat for security and order.

Dreams, Philosophy, Science and Fiction

This chapter informs contemporary readers and writers of experimental fiction of the developments in science, philosophy and psychology which influenced the modernist writer, so that they can utilize some of the ideas and practices into their own work.

What were the *new* developments in psychology during the modern times?

The most fundamental developments in psychology came from Sigmund Freud, 1856–1939. In his work *Interpretations of Dreams*, he explored the unconscious, believing it to be the 'true' reality. He was concerned with the following questions: Where do dreams come from? What causes a particular dream? Freud discovered that the hidden wish in dreams is often of a sexual nature. Repressed thoughts have to get past censorship before they can enter the dream world. Therefore, the function of dreams is to discharge repressed wishes.

Freud declared that the unconscious mind may be accessed through the analysis and interpretation of the individual's dreams. He explained that the seemingly illogical dream state is governed by a logic, with dream thoughts converted into content by processes of displacement (this is where the feelings related to one thing are connected to a different one; negative feelings towards one person are displaced onto something or someone else) and condensation (many ideas are blended together by the dream – implying that one image can stand for many associations). Freud provided a method for expressing the interior; this led to the breakdown of traditional values.

For Freud, the different parts of the mind were in a constant state of conflict. He suggested that the mind is divided into the id, or unconscious, the ego and the superego, and all human beings are the result of conflict between these three.

How did developments in psychology impact on the modern writer?

Many modernist writers were concerned with consciousness which can be traced to the influence of Freud and his work. And so, Freud's work impacted upon them considerably. As characters became more complex and contradictory, multi-voices, multi-layered narratives were the natural outcomes. The interior of characters' minds were explored. While Woolf concerned herself with the subconscious, Andre Breton, founder of surrealism, was interested in the theories of Freud; he recorded the dreams of men shell-shocked in the First World War. For Breton, Freud's theory of the unconscious allowed for another place beyond 'reality', a surreal place, a place of dreams, where the truth lies. He experimented with opening up the dream world through automatic writing, that is writing which is practised spontaneously, almost in a trance state, without engaging thought or censorship. He collaborated with Philippe Soupault to create *Magnetic Fields*, a work of automatic writing, considered to be the first surrealist work. The writers Ford Madox Ford, Proust, Conrad and Joyce, all explored the nature of sleep, dreams, reality and the unconscious in their work.

As Virginia Woolf stated, human character had changed and she cited December 1910 as the point of change; this, in part, had to do with the influence of Freud and developments in science and philosophy. Virginia Woolf, Elizabeth Drew and May Sinclair, who assisted in establishing a psychoanalytical clinic in London, and Dorothy Richardson, who reviewed books on psychoanalysis, were all writers keen to examine the mind in their fiction. Later, D. H. Lawrence, who was especially interested in a consciousness beyond thought and the nature of sexuality, explored the Oedipus complex in *Sons and Lovers* through the character Paul Morel and the relationship he has with his mother. For D. H. Lawrence, the unconscious was the most essential aspect of a human being. American writers also absorbed the developments in psychology and brought them back to the United

States, where they fired the imaginations of writers such as William Faulkner, who employed Freudian elements into his work.

Freud believed that the mind was a network of differing and conflicting drives; our thoughts are often scattered and conflicting and multiple, and so is our worldview; it isn't linear or always rational and ordered. The mind is a not a fixed place; it is in a state of flux, a process, an endless procession of shifting moments (Lehrer, p. 177). This is illustrated in *To the Lighthouse*: 'Such was the complexity of things … to feel violently two opposite things at the same time; that's what you feel, was one; that's what I feel, was the other, and then they fought together in her mind, as now' (Lehrer, p. 78).

What influence did psychology have on modernist writing techniques?

A feature of modernist writing was the use of symbols, influenced by Freud's *Interpretation of Dreams*; symbols in our dreams are said to stand in for or represent something. In fiction, symbols are characters, objects or colours chosen by the writer to represent concepts or ideas, for example, the lighthouse and the rainbow used by Virginia Woolf and D. H. Lawrence in their literary works. The lighthouse illustrated that nothing is ever only one thing and the rainbow has biblical implications. The rainbow is a symbol of peace. God showed Noah the rainbow when the flood was finally over.

Experiment with this: Learning to Experiment with Symbols in Fiction

Write a passage from a novel in which you use the following symbols: a rose and a clock. Consider what they represent and when, how and why you use them in the narrative.

What were the new developments in philosophy in modern times?

The German philosopher, composer and poet Friedrich Nietzsche's impact on modernism was complex. Nietzsche's ideas are considered to be as important as Freud's in terms of establishing an intellectual environment in which the modernist writers could thrive. Nietzsche's claim that God was dead had an impact upon the decline of religious faith even before the twentieth century; this was further accelerated by Charles Darwin's theories of *On the Origin of the Species*. Darwin demonstrated that species evolve through secular processes rather than divine intervention. Nietzsche rejected Christian morality and believed the truth was found by looking within. In addition, he embraced irrationalism over rationalism.

The essence of the French philosopher Henri Bergson was that intuition was more significant than science or rationalism for understanding reality. He was resistant to a mechanistic view of the universe. 'The laws of science were fine for inert matter...for discerning the relationships between atoms and cells, but us? We had a consciousness, a memory, a being... According to Bergson... – the reality of our self-consciousness could not be reduced or experimentally dissected. He believed that we could only understand ourselves through *intuition*, a process that required lots of introspection, time spent contemplating our inner connections' (Lehrer, p. 78). Clearly, we can see links here between Nietzsche's and Bergson's philosophies and modernist concerns.

How did Friedrich Nietzsche and Henri Bergson impact on the modern writer?

It has been suggested that the lack of an omniscient narrator in some modernist fiction was reflecting an era of declining religious beliefs and an ultimately all-seeing, all-knowing, ever-present God. As already stated, Nietzsche questioned all forms of ultimate authority or truth, believing that the irrational self was probably the most creative aspect of a human being. Modernist writers began to create worlds and characters in which the irrational were privileged.

Marcel Proust was influenced by the philosopher Henri Bergson. Proust's literature 'became a celebration of intuition' (p. 78). Proust's 'absorption of Bergson's philosophy led him to conclude that the nineteenth-century novel, with its privileging of things over thoughts, had everything exactly backward' (p. 78). Literary works which simply describe things, 'is in fact, although it calls itself realist, the furthest removed from reality' (p. 79). 'But how could a work of fiction demonstrate the power of intuition? How could a novel prove that it was, as Bergson put it, "ultimately spiritual and not physical"? ...'. This is how the Search begins, with the famous madeleine, out of which a mind unfolds:

> No sooner had the warm liquid mixed with the crumbs touched my palate than a shudder ran through me and I stopped, intent upon the extraordinary thing that was happening to me ... at once the vicissitudes of life had become indifferent to me ... It is plain that the truth I am seeking lies not in the cup but in myself.

Here we see the essence of Bergson's philosophy encapsulated.

What were the developments in science during modern times?

Changes in psychological thought were matched by changes in scientific theory. Previously Newton had showed that the universe obeyed precise rules or laws and that events as different as the motion of the planets around the sun and the bending of a light beam can be explained by the application of these rules. He believed in absolute time and absolute space; according to him, everything in the universe was predictable and simple laws were all that was required to understand how it functioned. In the Newton model of physics, there was only one reality at a time; all changes in the physical world were described in terms of a separate dimension called time; absolute-time-space co-ordinates were the framework for a fixed, predictable and law-abiding universe.

However, these rigid rules gave way to the world of Max Planck's quantum theory of 1900; it was a challenge to classical physics and suggested a contrasting worldview to the Newtonian model and a revision of the way reality was perceived. Quantum physics replaced the classical emphasis on separate parts. The quantum is 'An entangled universe, its many parts are interwoven, their boundaries and their identities overlap, and through their doing so a new reality is created' (Danah Zohar, The Quantum Society, p. 258). One of the most revolutionary ideas shown by quantum physics is that light is both 'wave-like' and 'particle-like' at the same time. In 1927, George Thompson proved the dual nature of electrons, known as the 'wave-particle duality'. Electric charge travels as waves but departs and arrives as particles and neither 'wave-like' nor the 'particle-like' properties is more 'real'. Virginia Woolf is ' ... enormously aware of time. Throughout her novels time clangs like fate; its sound reverberates with terrifying persistence. When Jacob, when Mrs Dalloway, when Orlando hear clocks strike, the explosion shakes the complex fabric of their being. The whole of *Orlando* is a fantasia on the time sense' (Holtby, pp. 52–3). Indeed, Woolf experiments with 'consciousness of time' (Memoir, p. 138) in sophisticated ways, weaving past with present; for example, in *Jacob's Room* the reader is able to observe a number of incidents happening simultaneously: Florinda sick, Jacob looking at his butterfly collection and recalling how he caught them, Clara asleep, Mrs Pasco watching the steamers along the Cornish coast and all the while: 'Each moment becomes enriched by other moments; consciousness is never simple' (Memoir, p. 139).

Einstein's *Theory of Relativity* illustrated that time was an illusion; it denied the existence of an absolute time: present, past and future all co-exist in space-time. Likewise the past is out there still. Time is not everywhere the same; however, it depends on how fast we are moving on an ever-turning globe, in an ever-changing universe. Such scientific discoveries changed the way people lived and thought about the nature of time; this also impacted upon the world of fiction.

Freud was also concerned with the nature of time; in his view, present and past are connected, though not necessarily chronologically. It was his belief that the past continues to exist in buried memories in the unconscious and that past events continue to shape one's personality. Indeed, childhood experiences can be closer to the present than more recent events, and, as such, are highly influential. As we have discovered, the way to recover the past, Freud claimed, was through dreams.

What writing techniques evolved to correspond with developments in science?

Many new writing techniques evolved to correspond with developments in science, such as disruption of conventional chronology, interior monologue, discontinuity and stream of consciousness. New forms were employed as writers experimented and explored these new theories that established that there is no absolute time. There are, however, different concepts of time: time happening in the mind and time happening on the clock. The modernist writers tended to favour the idea of time happening in the mind, which is unlimited and stretches over years, centuries even. They sought to abandon the arrangement of events in a linear time sequence favoured by traditional realist writers. In *Orlando*, for example, forty years is spread over three centuries, whereas in *Mrs Dalloway* the whole significance of fifty years is contained within twenty-four hours.

Time in the mind also involves the impact of memory; this is explored in Proust's *Remembrance of Things Past* in which Marcel's narrative is governed by the randomness of his memories, and as a result, this structures the novel. These memories are often involuntary, inspired by a smell or a taste which suffuses the mind with such a vivid sensation that he is taken back to an earlier version of himself. In particular, when he tastes a madeleine cake dipped in tea, he is taken back to his childhood; as already stated, the past is out there still.

Likewise in *Ulysses*, a book very much concerned with complicating ideas of form, Bloom's mind, when in Dublin for a day, flits back to his earlier life; Joyce uses stream of consciousness to recall past events which he juxtaposes with present events in time. For example, in Chapter 6, when Bloom is at Paddy Dignam's funeral, he moves back in memory to the burial of his son, the suicide of his father and to his life with Molly.

Ulysses is an example of a literary work which subverts the linear narrative; even sentences are fragmentary 'Cup of tea soon. Good. Mouth dry' (p. 65). Dorothy Richardson's *Pilgrimage* uses gaps in the layout to indicate the fractured nature of time.

Experiment with this: Learning to Experiment with Time in Fiction

Imagine a character who, in their dreams, has returned to the town where they lived as a child. Write a short story in which the character explores the town on foot; however, in their mind, they are moving forwards and backwards in time, exploring their memories of the place. Experiment with fragmented sentences and gaps in the layout too.

So it can be seen that science, philosophy and psychology suggested a world where absolutely nothing was absolute and once again this was reflected in the fiction of the modernist writers. As Proust's character Marcel states: 'the current philosophy of the day...it was agreed that...nothing was considered real and incontestable except the individual tastes of each person' (p. 304).

Further Reading

Cunningham, Michael (1999) The Hours, London: Fourth Estate.

Dickens, Charles (2010) Great Expectations, London: Harper Press.

Faulkner, William (1995) The Sound and the Fury, London: Vintage Classic.

Holtby, Winifred (2007) Virginia Woolf: A Critical Memoir, London: Continuum.

Jackson, Kevin (2012) Constellations ff Genius: 1922: Modernism Year One, London: Hutchinson.

Jones, Gail (2011) Five Bells, London: Harvill Secker.

—— (2007) Dubliners, London: Penguin Classics.

Joyce, James (2010) Ulysses, London: Wordsworth Editions.

Lawrence, D. H. (1997) Sons and Lovers, London: Wordsworth Editions.

—— (2005) Lady Chatterley's Lover, London: Wordsworth Editions.

—— (2008) Women in Love, London: Vintage Classic.

Lehrer, Jonah (2011) Proust Was a Neuroscientist, Edinburgh: Canongate.

McGregor, Jon (2011) If Nobody Speaks of Remarkable Things, London: Bloomsbury.

Morgan, Clare (2011) A Book For All and None, London: Weidenfeld & Nicolson.

Poust, Marcel (2006) Remembrance of Things Past, London: Wordsworth Editions.

Pykett, Lyn (1995) Engendering Fictions, London: Hodder Headline.

Richardson, Dorothy (2000) Pilgrimage, Madison: University Of Wisconsin Press.

Sackville, Amy (2010) The Still Point, London: Portobello.

—— (2013) Orkney, London: Granta.

Self, Will (2013) Umbrella, London: Bloomsbury Paperbacks.

Stevenson, Randall (1998) Modernist Fiction, Essex: Pearson Education.

Tew, Phillips and Murray, Alex (2009) The Modernist Handbook, London: Continuum.

Wilson, Leigh (2007) Modernism, London: Continuum.

Woolf, Virginia (1976) Mrs Dalloway, London: Triad Grafton Books.

—— (1994) To the Lighthouse, London: Wordsworth Editions.

—— (2008) Jacob's Room, London: Tark Classic Fiction.

Section Two

When Were/Who Were the Beats?

When were the Beats?

The name 'Beat' was originally invented by Jack Kerouac in 1948. The movement stretched to the mid-1960s; however, it had its zenith in the 1950s.

After the worldwide depression of the 1930s and 1940s and the devastation that had occurred throughout the world – for example, Dresden, Hiroshima and Pearl Harbour – millions of people from the 1950s and 1960s generations hoped for prosperity and stability. However, ensuing peace treaties gave way to 'Cold War' as the two superpowers, the United States and the Soviet Union, contended with each other for ideological world power. The launch of *Sputnik 1*, the first artificial satellite, into space in 1957 by the Soviet Union was considered to be a major milestone of the Cold War; the United States reaction was to launch an *Explorer*, three months later, thus kick-starting the space race.

The post-war years, the time in which the Beats emerged, bore witness to a number of changes – economic, political, cultural and social – which shaped their lifestyle choices and writing practices. Indeed, these changes, for example, communist crusades and the rise of McCarthyism, a practice of making unfair allegations or using unfair investigative techniques resulting in 'witch hunts' and 'black lists' for alleged communist activities, in turn led to widespread fear and paranoia throughout the United States. McCarthyism was named after Joseph McCarthy, a senator who made accusations that more than two hundred communists had infiltrated the United States government (this was later proved to be untrue). This was a widespread phenomenon, affecting all levels of society, in particular government employees, union activists, educators, entertainers and writers.

During this era, there was also the civil rights struggle, the rise of feminism, the threat of annihilation from nuclear weapons and the development of popular culture. All these led to a complex new chapter in world history, which provided a climate ripe for experimentation in all art forms.

With the trauma of the Second World War in the past, this was a time of economic growth and a large-scale expansion of the middle classes, which perpetuated the concept of the 'American Suburban Dream'. The 1950s was a period of conformity, an era which was considered to be both socially conservative and highly materialistic in nature. Consumerism became a key component of society, with buying trends being influenced by many American cultural and economic aspects such as advertising and the widespread availability of bank loans.

There was a resurgence of evangelical Christianity, for example, The Billy Graham Evangelistic Association. It was a time of taboos, and attitudes to sex and censorship were prudish. However, a new consciousness was rising in terms of race and equality. The civil rights movement with key figures such as Martin Luther King, Rosa Parks and Malcolm began fighting for profound change, insisting on the rights for all Americans to an equal education, regardless of race, creed or religion.

Socially and culturally, many developments were apparent during the 1950s, for example, three quarters of the population purchased their first television; quiz shows such as *What's My Line* and *Westerns* became popular, thus propelling movie stars such as John Wayne and Roy Rogers to fame. Indeed, movies were celebrated throughout this period, with the likes of Marilyn Monroe and James Dean becoming glamorous movie star sensations. In addition, a number of television shows were produced, which portrayed a romanticized view of middle-class life, for example, *Father Knows Best*. Comic book audiences grew.

Characters such as *Flash Gordon*, *Peanuts* and *Dennis the Menace* were amongst the favourites. Science fiction and superman comics were in abundance, too. Music flourished, especially jazz, popular and country music, and then, in the mid-1950s, Rock-n-Roll emerged, Elvis Presley being the superstar of the period. In terms of high art, the focus for artistic practice switched from Paris to New York with the advent of artistic Abstract Expressionism.

And so, for the middle-class Americans living through the 1950s, life was more secure, prosperous and culturally rich than the previous years. However, it was a lifestyle vehemently rejected by the Beats, in favour of a very different one.

Who were the Beats?

The Beat Generation, then, was a term used to describe a group of American writers who came to prominence in the 1950s, writers who provided a counter-culture to Cold War politics and a social commentary on the hip youth culture of the 1950s, both of which they captured in their experimental writing practice.

Although the philosophy of the Beats was considered to be anti-academic, the seeds for the Beat movement were sown in an academic environment, as they originally met at Columbia University in the early 1940s. This was where the charismatic Lucien Carr and Allen Ginsberg, following nights of drinking and reading works such as *Seasons in Hell* by the nineteenth-century poet Arthur Rimbaud (whom Carr considered to be a doppelganger), discussed the need for a *new vision* for art. This vision was not formulated with intellectual rigour. However, it was agreed that art must view the world in a new light, one not restricted by convention or repression, but one that strived for unmediated self-expression and produced literature that was experimental and took risks.

Lucien Carr introduced Allen Ginsberg to William S. Burroughs, a Harvard graduate, whose childhood friend was David Kammerer, an English teacher and a physical education instructor at Washington University. Kammerer originally met Lucien Carr when he was his Boy Scout leader in St Louis and soon became infatuated with him. Edie Parker, another member of the group, introduced Carr to her then boyfriend Jack Kerouac.

Jack Kerouac, Allen Ginsberg and William S. Burroughs were known as the three musketeers of the Beat Generation, although a number of other writers were also considered to be part of the Beats; these included the already mentioned, Lucien Carr, David Kammerer, Neal Cassady, Gregory Corso and John Clellon Holme.

In the mid-1950s, the main figures associated with the Beats, with the exception of William Burroughs, gathered in San Francisco, because of its reputation as being a centre of creativity. Here they became friends with the 'San Francisco Renaissance', a term used to describe groups of avant-garde American writers emerging at the end of the Second World War. These writers, who included Kenneth Rexroth, Lawrence Ferlinghtti, Lew Welch, Gary Snyder and Kirby Doyle, embraced performing and visual arts, philosophy and Asian culture. They were joined by Tuli Kuperberg and Philip Lamantia, who were members of the Black Mountain College, looking for a new creative community, and later by Bob Kaufman, who was considered the first person to be called a *beatnik*.

What were the Beats rebelling against?

The adjective *beat* came to the group of writers through underworld association with Herbert Huncke, a drug addict and thief who met Burroughs in 1946 and introduced the members of the Beats to the junky lifestyle and the language associated with this lifestyle, including the word *beat*. *Beat* originally implied *beaten down* and *tired*. However, Jack Kerouac expanded the meaning of the term by adding the paradoxical association *upbeat* and the musical association *on the beat*.

By associating with people considered to be living on the margins of society, the Beats were rebelling against Cold War politics and the conservative values of the time. Even though they were well educated and generally from middle-class backgrounds, the Beats renounced capitalism, seeing it as being destructive to the human spirit and antithetical to social equality. In addition, they were rebelling against the strong sexual taboos of mass culture and set out to push back boundaries and indulge in experimentation with sexual practices, drug taking and spiritual transcendence. Consequently, as will be seen in subsequent chapters, some of their work, which explored their views and lifestyles, for example, *Naked Lunch* by William Burroughs, was deemed highly controversial. *Naked Lunch*, a travelogue of depravity with an underlying theme of addiction, drawn from Burroughs' own sexual and drug-taking experiences in New York City, Mexico and Tangier and the dream-like interzone, structured in 'routines', was intended to be read in any order.

The novel was published by European publishers, Olympia Press in Paris in 1959, but the United States obscenity laws prevented it from being published until 1962; the work was then banned and was eventually repealed in 1966. This was deemed a win for free speech.

What inspired the Beats?

Whilst engaging in experimental writing practice, the Beats took inspiration from a variety of sources. Several of them claimed that the Romantic poets were a major influence on their work, whereas others claimed to be inspired by modernism and surrealism, especially Andre Breton's automatic writing and cut-ups. Also, the American Transcendental Movement of the nineteenth century was said to be a powerful source of inspiration for the Beats: the writer of poetry and prose Henry David Thoreau being revered as a symbol of protest.

Romanticism

Gregory Corso, in particular, was influenced by Percy Shelley. Indeed, he was so inspired by the works of Shelley that he was buried at the foot of his grave in Rome. Allen Ginsberg was also influenced by Shelley; his famous work *Howl* was compared with Shelley's poem *Queen Mab*. Both political and philosophical epic poems referred to other-worldly creatures – angels and fairies – and shared a hallucinatory quality encapsulated in the language. In addition, the two works set out to liberate humanity from conformity and oppression. John Keats was also a source of inspiration for Ginsberg; he mentioned Shelley's *Adonais* at the beginning of *Kaddish* and cited it as a major influence on his work. However, he was mostly inspired by William Blake, who he saw as a prophet. After graduating from Columbia in 1948 and moving to New York City, Ginsberg felt isolated; he spoke of a vision he had during this time, one in which he heard his own voice reciting Blake's poetry. Ginsberg spoke of this incident as a revelation, one which represented a turning point in his spiritual development.

Modernism

The Beats were also inspired by some of the modernist poets like Ezra Pound and William Carlos Williams and prose writers like James Joyce. Williams encouraged the Beats to speak with an American voice, rather than imitating European poetic voices and forms; he was a mentor to Ginsberg, both men originating from Paterson, New Jersey.

Surrealism

Andre Breton's automatic writing style and cut-ups inspired the Beats. Carl Solomon introduced the work of Breton to Ginsberg, and this had a profound influence on *Kaddish*. The poetry of Greg Corso was influenced by surrealist poetry; like the surrealists, he experimented by using dream-like images and random juxtaposition of dissociated images in his work.

What additional influences encouraged the Beats to experiment with the content of their writing?

In addition to the romantic, surrealist and modernist artistic practices, the Beats had other influences, such as the natural world, city life and travel, that affected their writing. Also, they related and interacted with a mix of cultures, but fundamentally a great deal of their work was influenced by Eastern religions and altered states of consciousness; this was not so apparent in terms of the form of their writing, but it was more in terms of the content.

Another influence on the Beats was music, especially jazz, and like their musician heroes, for example, Charlie Parker, they too adopted bohemian lifestyles, ones of social rebellion, influenced by drug and sexual experimentation, in terms of both heterosexual and homosexual practices; this sexual experimentation inspired the use of graphic sexual language and hugely affected the content of their work which pushed back the boundaries of acceptability and ultimately censorship. And so, along with their rebellious, nomadic lifestyles and their controversial writing practice, the Beats were deemed as outcasts. However, much of their work has stood the test of time: *Howl, Naked Lunch, On the Road*; this is because of the quality of the writing and the content of the works which has universal intrigue and appeal and is still highly relevant to readers and writers of experimental fiction in the twenty-first century.

How did their influences impact upon the form, techniques and style of the Beats' writing?

The Beats' writing style was fast-paced, energetic, emotional and confessional in tone, similar to jazz. Like the jazz musicians, the Beats experimented with improvisation. The process of writing can be related to that of a journey; the actual *ride* was as imperative as the arrival, that is, the completed work. A technique known as stream of consciousness was used by the Beats. Jack Kerouac aspired to *consciousness on the page*, which led to a form of writing which disregarded paragraphs, punctuation and sometimes linearity; it was a spontaneous, free-flowing writing practice, one that contemporary experimental writers have much to learn from. Indeed, the various forms, styles and techniques employed by the Beats – for example, free talking, free voices, freedom of expression, dream-like, random juxtaposition of dissociated images, cut-ups, non-linear texts, use of slang, confessional, passionate tone, hallucinatory atmosphere, stream of consciousness, hybrid forms of work that refuse rigidity, as well as political critique that drives the work – will be explored in the next section of this book, so that readers who wish to learn from the experimental forms and techniques of the Beats can do so; in addition, writers can utilize this rebellious, exciting and innovative practice within their own creative writing.

Beat/Music

This chapter illustrates how jazz was inspiring for the Beat movement, especially in terms of its improvisational element, so that readers can learn from this experimental technique and apply it to their own writing. In addition, it explores how the counter culture shift in terminology came about from *beatnik* to *hippie*.

How did jazz influence the Beat writers?

As the Beat movement was getting underway, the form of music known as *Bebop* was making a profound impact, especially in New York, where 5th Street was alive and buzzing with jazz clubs: The Open Door, Red Door and Minton's were amongst the most famous and frequented. *Bebop* was an innovative style of jazz, focusing on virtuosity; it was associated with musicians such as Charlie Parker, Thelonious Monk, Max Roach and Dizzy Gillespie. Kerouac, Ginsberg and fellow Beats spent much of their time in clubs *digging the jazz* and *shooting the breeze*, enjoying listening to the music, socializing, smoking and drinking. They were known as 'hipsters', the ones who were 'cool' and adopted the jazz musician's way of life. Jazz players were people who the Beats identified with as they sought to marginalize themselves from mainstream society; they considered them romantic figures: living on the margins, outcasts of white society, talented and tormented, but passionate about their art. And so, the Beats talked the talk of jazz, took the drugs the musicians took, drank heavily and had colourful sex lives like their *secret heroes*, who, in turn, modelled themselves on the French poet Arthur Rimbaud. Rimbaud had lived a decadent life but one that was nevertheless committed to his art, so much so that he burnt himself out whilst still very young. The Beats and jazz players lived their art and lived by their ideals; they collapsed the distance between life and art, but for some, for example, Jack Kerouac, that also meant burning out before he reached old age.

Many terms from the jazz culture were *borrowed* by the Beats and used in their writing, for example, *dig* and *square*; it is difficult to translate directly the obscure language of the jazz musicians adopted by the Beats. However, dig meant really like 'hot jazz' finding it 'cool', whereas square implied dull and conformist, in other words boring.

Jazz became the inspiration behind the Beats experimental writing in both form and content. Kerouac often referred to jazz as being the greatest discovery of his life. The connection with the improvisational jazz musicians became the impetus for the free-flowing, spontaneous prose he was trying to create. He endeavoured to follow the creative process behind jazz and apply it to his writing, namely free association of thought, abandonment of formal structures and spontaneity of composition; this brought writing closer to the spoken word.

And so, *Bebop* improvisation was the technique the Beats used to approach their creative process of writing. They used the principles of *Bebop* playing and applied it to prose and poetry, a style sometimes referred to as *Bop Prosody*, for example, in *Book of Blues* – which was considered by the publisher Lawrence Ferlinghetti to be more prose than poetry – Kerouac copies the style of jazz by repeating phrases:

I got the San Francisco Blues
Bluer than misery
I got the San Francisco Blues
Bluer than eternity
I gotta go on home
Fine me
Another
Sanity

(*Book of Blues*, San Francisco Blues 36th chorus)

Just as the jazz player used the control and bursts of breath to play notes, the Beat writers employed the same technique with language, so steams of consciousness, gaps in the text, lack of punctuation became their distinctive writing style, and the rhythm and intensity of emotion within the writing mirrored that of jazz, as in *Doctor Sax* (Book 4, 117):

> And not that tragic halo,
> Half git, half hidden-
> The night the man with
> The watermelon died-should I
> Tell-(Oh Ya Ya Yoi Yoi)
> How he died

Experiment with this: Learning to Create Writing that Mirrors Jazz

Write a novel extract

Imagine you are one of The Beats in a club listening to jazz and engaging in conversation. Use your senses and emotions to capture this experience in your writing, repeat phrases, incorporate bursts of language and then create gaps in the text, a text that tries to capture the spoken word. Now do further research into musicians, jazz clubs, fashion, language used during the 1950s. Rewrite your text, still retaining the form of the narrative, but inscribing it with authentic detail of the time.

What was a beatnik?

The term *beatnik* was coined by Herb Caen of the San Francisco Chronicle on 2 April 1958 in response to the recent Russian satellite Sputnik and Beat Generation. This suggested that the beatniks were *far out* of the mainstream society and pro-Communist. The Beatniks were renowned for their distinctive *look*; they wore dark shades, sandals, black pants, turtleneck sweaters and sported goatee beards.

What is/was a hippie?

During the late 1950s, aspects of the Beat movement transformed into the sixties Counter Culture Movement: the hippies. The hippies shared the rebellious nature of the beatniks and were anti-establishment and defied middle-class values. They were also against the Vietnam War, believing strongly in love, peace, freedom and understanding. Allen Ginsberg was involved with the hippies and the anti-war movement. However, Jack Kerouac parted company with Ginsberg during this time and was openly critical of the protest movements.

Rather than jazz, the hippies were fans of the Beatles, in particular John Lennon, who wrote *Give Peace a Chance*, and George Harrison, who embraced Eastern spirituality; he wrote 'My Sweet Lord' and studied sitar in India with Ravi Shankar. Other musicians the hippies followed were The Doors, Jimi Hendrix and Bob Dylan. In contrast to the dark clothing worn by the beatniks, the hippie wore colourful psychedelic tops, scarves, jeans, beads and grew their hair long.

Experiment with this: Learning to Write Characters: The Beatnik and the Hippie

Write a novel extract in which two characters, a beatnik and a hippie, meet at a party. In your extract, give their first impressions of each other. Write a conversation in which they discuss their views on politics and taste in music. Draw on historical facts and cite specific music and musicians, ensuring you create credible voices for your characters by employing the appropriate language to render the text authentic.

Spirituality and the Beats

This chapter investigates the spiritual yearnings of the Beats, the profound influence Buddhism had on the writers, both in terms of content of their writing and their creative writing process, so that contemporary writers can experiment with these ideas and techniques too.

Which spiritual writers informed the Beats?

Aware of the spiritual bankruptcy of Europe, following the First World War, many writers turned to the wisdom of the East. Henry Miller, considered to be the great grandfather of the Beats, was such a writer. He was admired by the Beats and the hippies for his rebellious streak, his 'Do what thou wilt' philosophy. Miller had a fascination with the East, in particular Zen and Tao. This fascination manifested itself in his studies and in his writing. In 1942, he wrote his spiritual travelogue *The Colossus of Maroussi*.

English writer Aldous Huxley also turned to the East. His spiritual search was born out of his pacifism. Through his study of the factors leading up to the First World War, and influences preparing Europe for another one, he came to the conclusion that society would be worthless if there weren't changes in people. He read *Vedanta*, the teachings of the *Vedas*, the earliest Indian scriptures, often referred to as the Upanishads; *Bhagavad Gita; Tao Te Ching* and Sufi writings. In 1932, Huxley wrote *Brave New World*, a novel set in the future. The theme of *Brave New World* was the advancement of science as it affects human beings; it explored developments in reproductive technology, psychological manipulation and the fear of loss of individual identity. As a result of further study of Eastern mysticism, and his experimentation with mescaline, Huxley published *The Doors of Perception* in 1954. The novel took its title from a phrase in the William Blake poem *The Marriage of Heaven and Hell* and was a documentation of his drug trip and the insights and visions he had. As a result of taking mescaline, Huxley understood the nature of reality from a Buddhist perspective: an individual was not independent and separate from the world nor was reality outside one's self; God was to be found within, and our individual consciousness was only a small part of a vast psychic sea he called *Mind at Large*; in Buddhist terms everything is connected. The teachings of the East were both an inspiration and a comfort to Huxley; he turned to the *Tibetan Book of the Dead*, a work of tantric Buddhism, as his wife, Maria, was dying of cancer.

German-born, Swiss poet, novelist and painter Herman Hess received the Nobel Prize in literature in 1946. He was like the Beats, a rebel, an outsider, a man who revolted against materialism and the decline of culture. Inspired by Buddha, he was concerned with the individual's inner journey to discover one's true self and overcome suffering, by listening to one's inner voice. Consequently, his literary works were steeped with Eastern philosophy and were a record of this spiritual journey to a place within. The works of Hess, for example, *Steppenwolf*, *Siddhartha* and *The Glass Bead Game*, all explored an individual's search for self-knowledge and spirituality and informed the work of the Beats. Hess wrote one of the most influential works of European literature in the twentieth century: *Siddhartha*, the novel still has wide appeal. As mentioned, the focus of the novel was the spiritual development of the characters, altered states of consciousness and the mystical aspects. Hess was a pacifist who studied Eastern and Western philosophy, in particular the *Upanishads* and the *Bhagavad Gita*, works that greatly informed *Siddhartha*, a novel which captured the quest of the Brahmin Siddhartha, a quest to conquer his fears and suffering, despite temptations of wealth, luxury and those of the flesh, in order to attain transcendental bliss, the purpose of human existence, a concept familiar to anyone who takes the Buddhist path and who is familiar with the Eastern texts.

The *Upanishads* are said to be divine revelations received by seers. *Upanishad* is a Sanskrit word suggesting 'sitting down under', that is, at the feet of an enlightened teacher. The *Upanishads*, therefore, are teachings received in this way; their purpose is more concerned with inspiration rather than instruction, but it is not known who composed them or when. The focus of the *Upanishads* is that the reality of God is not something separate from an individual, but it is the innermost part of one's being, one's highest self, known as Brahman, Self or Atman.

The *Bhagavad Gita* is one of the classic spiritual texts of the world which enshrines the essential values of the *Upanishad*. The story concerns the plight of Arjuna, the commander of an army, who after seeing his kith and kin on the opposing side of a pending war tells Krishna, his spiritual guide, that he will not fight, as he is overcome by pity. Krishna replies with concerns not just about the war, but the ones that concern humanity: Why do we exist? Why is there suffering? The structure of the narrative is question and answer, its intent enquiry and its goal self-discovery and enlightenment.

The spiritual development of the characters, the journey within, was the focus of the novel *Siddhartha*, not plot. As a consequence of reading the Eastern texts, Hess discovered the truth seeker rises above the temptations of the senses. This was a theme of his other influential work *Steppenwolf* too. In the *Upanishads*, the conflict of duality was described as that between the 'higher' and 'lowers' selves. The 'lower self' comprising the senses turns to the transient, sensual world of pleasure, known as *sansara*, whereas the mind can turn inward and discover the 'higher self' which is blissful, a realm where duality does not exist. Hess illustrated the theme of duality in the novel by the role of two friends of Siddhartha, firstly Govinda and later Vasudeva. The protagonist Siddhartha was said to represent Hess, and the friends were said to represent who he wished to become.

Another writer inspired by Hess was the poet T. S. Eliot who was born in the United States but moved to England and was made a British subject. Eliot was awarded the Nobel Prize for literature in 1948. His most famous work is the poem *The Waste Land*. In May 1922 T. S. Eliot visited Hess in Montagnola. Hesse's essay *In Sight of Chaos* (1919) was mentioned in the notes of *The Waste Land*, with references to the Occult, Tarot and *Upanishads*, and mystical symbols.

Experiment with this: Learning to Use a Spiritual Quest

Create a character who is making a journey to recover or find something of spiritual value. What is (s)he wanting to recover? Why? Write the journey including a series of obstacles and characters who help them overcome these obstacles along the way. Focus on the inner journey of the character and their spiritual development as well as the outer journey.

In what ways were the Beats spiritual?

The media, and indeed the FBI, saw the rebellious Beats as being a threat to middle-class, conservative society. However, despite their frenetic lifestyles, the writings of the Beats were profoundly spiritual and transcendental. The Beats' philosophy was one of anti-materialism and stressed the importance of bettering one's inner self over and above material possessions.

The German philosopher Oswald Spengler wrote *The Decline of The West*; this text discussed the rise and fall of civilization. In 1945 Burroughs gave Jack Kerouac a copy of this text. Spengler suggested that it was within the cultures of the East where a person may discover one's spiritual path; this text no doubt inspired Jack to see beyond the consumer culture of 1950s. Spengler suggested that those who are downbeat will prevail when social structures collapse.

So, although, Jack Kerouac's *On the Road* was about true-life stories, and made up ones, whilst making road trips and living out of a car, it was fundamentally a spiritual quest, a search for meaning. The spiritual quest which was the focus of the book was interior; however, the trials and tribulations faced actually on the road, coupled with the beauty of the landscape, accentuated the spiritual journey. *On the Road*, although a spiritual quest, was also considered to be about the search for the lost brother, father and also Kerouac himself, a book in which he was waiting for God to show himself, as he was known to say. Indeed, the Beats were asking big questions about human life and (wo)man's place within the universe. They were on a spiritual quest: beat to beatitude; suffering to joy; misery and sin to enlightenment and blessedness.

Kerouac was very much aware of his own mortality and life's impermanence, a concept he explored in *Visions of Cody*; he wrote that death was going to happen to us all sooner or later. Change and the impermanence of all things is the central teaching of Buddha. Buddhism, therefore, offers a method of practice that brings the individual into realization and alignment with the basic characteristic of reality, that is, its impermanence. Buddhism teaches that because we desire life to be permanent, death haunts us; fear of death has to be faced and integrated into our lives. It is imperative, according to Buddhism, that we come to terms with impermanence and free ourselves from the stress of what we are going to lose, because impermanence is our essence.

Buddhism teaches that one cannot avoid and ignore the darker parts of ourselves; this was something that the Beats were aware of, and indeed, to a certain extent, they celebrated this dark side of themselves and others in their writing. In addition, Buddhism emphasizes death in order to bring the urgency of life more vividly into focus, and the Beats too were concerned with the urgency of life which they expressed in their lifestyles and through their writing. They were also propelled on their spiritual journeys by their own suffering too. Most of the Beats were deeply troubled individuals. When he was four years old, Kerouac lost his brother, Gerald, as a result of a heart condition. He also lost his father when still young. William Burroughs's father shot and killed his mother when he was a child; his father later died as a result of his alcoholism and drug addiction. Ginsberg, too, had a traumatic life and spent some time in a mental hospital. And yet, the Beats wrote honestly and freely about suffering, and in so doing, they showed empathy and compassion.

The Beats were possibly motivated by the suffering of those who lived on the margins of society, too, for example, drug addicts, prostitutes, the homeless. Jack Kerouac, in particular, spent time exploring African-American culture among the clubs of Harlem. The idea of suffering or *dukkha* is central to the Buddhist philosophy which acknowledges that suffering is inevitable and a universal human experience. However, according to the Buddhist worldview, individuals should not avoid experiencing suffering, rather it is to be seen as something to be entered into, and, by doing so, we deepen our understanding of it, and ourselves, eventually moving through it. Buddhism teaches compassion towards others and ourselves. The basis of compassion or *metta* is loving-kindness; compassion arises when it comes into contact with suffering. It is a loving-kindness that one seeks to develop through the practice of mindful meditation. And within compassion there is always the opportunity for creative action, which, according to Buddhism, is a meaningful and purposeful way to live one's life.

In 1954, Jack Kerouac discovered Dwight Goddard's *A Buddhist Bible* at the San Jose Library. This marked the beginning of his fascination into Buddhism. Jack promoted the Washington state poet Gary Snyder as the Beats' spiritual guide, and he fictionalized him as Japhy Ryder in *Dharma Bums*, a book which also contained accounts of a mountain climbing trip Kerouac took with Snyder. In *Dharma Bums*, the character Ray Smith, who may be likened to Kerouac himself, wrestled with Buddhism and struggled to subdue his sexual desires. Japhy Ryder, however, did not chastise himself; he displayed *metta* and did not see pleasure as being in conflict with his spirituality. The *Dharma Bums* recalled the peaceful living together with Buddhist values that Kerouac and Snyder experienced in 1956 in Cabin Mill Valley.

Whilst studying Buddhism, Kerouac kept a journal containing poems, notes on Buddhism, while all the time he was trying to teach his mind compassion, peace and emptiness, through the art of meditation.

The *Diamond Sutra* was the most important Buddhist text for Kerouac. He studied the sutra, hoping to condition his mind to emptiness and to enlightenment. Kerouac was inspired by reading Henry David Thoreau's book *Walden*. Thoreau, a nineteenth-century philosopher and transcendentalist (transcendentalism is the prioritising of the spiritual over the material), explained how simple living was the key to enlightenment. Like Thoreau and the poet and transcendentalist Walt Whitman, the Beats looked for spirituality in nature, themselves and the East. Indeed, Kerouac lived alone for sixty-three days in a forest cabin on Desolation Peak, part of the North Cascade mountain range. He had a job there as a fire lookout, inspired by Snyder's accounts of his experiences as a lookout, but mainly it was Kerouac's idea to experience solitude, have visions and ultimately become enlightened. And he said of writing, that it's a 'silent meditation even though you're going hundred miles an hour…visions are only obtainable in silence and meditation' (*The Art of Fiction*, Kerouac, Paris Review, 1968).

Experiment with this: Learning How Meditation Inspires Creative Practice

Using your unconscious mind…

Sit in a quiet place. Close your eyes. Connect with your breath. Breathe in slowly through your nose and breathe out slowly through your nose. Allow thoughts to pass through your mind as if they are clouds floating by. Open your eyes. Write down the thoughts you had.

Close your eyes again. Connect with the breath. Imagine your mind is a still pond. Dive into it. What images and visions come to you? Open your eyes. Pick up a pen. Write freely about all that you have seen and felt.

Using your conscious mind…

Create a context in which your meditation experience can exist. Do not censor what you write, just write!

Now re-draft your piece of writing.

What spiritual practice did the Beats apply to their writing?

In addition to the content of the Beats' work being fused with Buddhist ideals, the techniques they employed in terms of their creative writing process, in particular the idea of freeing consciousness on to the page, relate to notions of non-attachment in Buddhism, otherwise known as *Aparigraha*. According to Buddhism, a common pattern of human behaviour is to resist change by clinging to 'desires' such as people, emotions, ways of seeing and responding to the world, material possessions, past conditioning, experiences, in an attempt to gain security. Therefore, one has difficulty living freely, accepting change and moving on with life. If one is attached, one's way of perceiving reality can be the result of many unconscious habits and actions, which are often repeated mechanically without question or insight; this is known as *samskara*. Non-attachment is the conscious realization that all 'desires' are under the control of the will. When one is able to harness the will and focus the mind, one is on a journey of self-study, known as *swadhyaya*, which leads to self-realization. Through adopting non-attachment techniques, the Beats were able to free their consciousness to the page. To the Beats, the old forms of fiction, for example, those of likes of Jane Austen and Henry Fielding, obscured meaning and stopped them getting to what really mattered, passion, energy, freedom, the rawness and reality of the actual experience. They wanted to write the truth, to let everything pour out in a rush, a stream of consciousness, without pausing to censor or use punctuation; in this way, they would arrive at the essence of meaning, the intensity of the experience.

The Sutras - meaning threads - written by Patanjali to tell a story are concerned with the search for inner balance through self-knowledge. According to the Sutras, non-attachment emerges from a mystical state, a trance, where it is natural to improvise and create and go with the flow; it is about being receptive to whatever comes up, being non-judgemental and detached, which is not the same as being disinterested. This process is about being absorbed in the moment as were the Beats when they wrote, in particular Jack Kerouac when he wrote *On the Road*, which will be explored in a later chapter. They gave themselves over to the writing and were not constrained by rules or structures; they were not concerned by the blank page. In Buddhism, the concept of emptiness is central to the philosophy. Emptiness is not nothingness, but it is the beginning of everything. Something can come from nothing.

Experiment with this: Learning to Use Non-attachment in Writing

Using this as a starting point for writing: I am loving the freedom…

Write! Do not be concerned with paragraphs or punctuation. Simply allow the words to flow from your mind onto the page and go with the flow of writing. Do not censor yourself, just trust the process and your unconscious mind. Be in the present moment. Improvise and create. Later, you may see connections between what now seem to be unrelated ideas, words and images, but for now just open up to your writing that will, if you let it, come naturally. Do not be constrained by rules and structures. Do not pontificate. Do not struggle for ideas, do not angst over the mechanics of the writing. Let the writing flow like clear water. Do not be inhibited. Do not worry about writing *well*. Do not strive for perfection. Keep the pen on the page and, keep your hand moving, keep writing for fifteen minutes or more if you can.

Sexuality, Drug Culture and Fiction

This chapter explores how sexual experimentation, drug taking and criminal behaviour impacted upon the form and content of the Beat fiction so that contemporary writers can enhance their own fiction by experimenting with these techniques.

What content informed the Beats' experimental writing practice?

The Beats rejected the mainstream values of America and were drawn to its underside, where there were drug addicts, prostitutes and swindlers. The content of the Beats' work, therefore, was highly influenced by the *dark side* of society and much of their writing takes the reader on a journey into this *darkness*. They were rebelling against *normality* and the prudish attitudes towards sex that existed in the conservative 1950s. To a certain extent, their literary works were a rage against a system that demanded conformity.

Jack Kerouac, William Burroughs and Allen Ginsberg had all been in prison and mental hospital. Neal Cassady was notorious for car theft, but was held in high esteem by the Beats for his passion for Zen. Indeed, *On the Road* is Cassady and Kerouac's experience of the decadent journey from New York to California, along the way they descend into one excess after another. As noted, David Kammerer had a fixation on Lucien Carr and pursued him so incessantly that in 1944 in Riverside Park this culminated in Carr stabbing Kammerer, tying his limbs with shoelaces, putting rocks in his pockets and rolling him into the Hudson River. Carr pleaded guilty to manslaughter and was sent to the Elmira Reformatory. The stabbing was an incident that Kerouac fictionalized in *The Town and the City* and later in *Vanity Duluoz*. In fact, most of the Beats fictionalized their lives, and as already mentioned, Burroughs fictionalized and romanticized his dark experiences too in *Naked Lunch*, a semi-autobiographical novel which is concerned with his life as a drug user and dealer of junk, heroin.

In addition to his drug habit, Burroughs had an interest in experimenting with criminal activity and made contacts with the criminal underworld of New York. Burroughs met Herbert Huncke, a criminal and drug addict, who hung about in Times Square. The Beats found him a fascinating and inspiring character; they felt that Huncke, a member of the underclass, had things to teach them as they had been sheltered by their middle-class upbringings. Ginsberg stashed stolen goods for Huncke, which led to him being arrested following a police car chase. He pleaded insanity and was briefly committed to Bellvue Hospital, where he met Carl Solomon. After Solomon's release, he became the contact which led to the publishing contract of Burrough's novel *Junky*, which was published in 1953.

How did content affect the language of the Beats writing?

The Beats used harsh language, slang and expletives within their literature to reflect the harsh reality that they were exploring, and they cited the American poet, father of free verse and journalist, Walt Whitman as being an influence on their work. *Wild Boys* by William Burroughs, for example, a novel set in an apocalyptic late twentieth century, depicted a gay youth culture whose goal was the downfall of western society. The language of this novel was graphic and visceral, strangely poetic and contained powerful visual imagery.

> The camera is the eye of a cruising vulture flying over an area of scrub, rubble and unfinished buildings on the outskirts of Mexico City.
>
> Five story building now walls no stairs...squatters have set up makeshift houses...floors are connected by ladders...dogs bark, chickens cackle, a boy on the roof makes a jack-off gesture as the camera sails past.

Close to the ground we see the shadow of our wings, dry cellars choked with thistles, rusty iron rods spouting like metal plants from cracked concrete, a broken bottle in the sun, shit-stained colour comics, an Indian boy against a wall with his knees up eating an orange sprinkled with red pepper. (*Wild Boys*, p. 1)

Experiment with this: Learning to Experiment with Language and Images

Like the opening of this extract, have a camera scanning a scene of your choice. Document what the camera sees. Experiment with the sound and texture of words, be creative and imaginative, and include alliteration and strong visual images in your writing.

Why did the Beats experiment with sexuality?

The Beats used sexual experimentation as a means to altered states of consciousness and a way of living life to the full and to discover what it meant to be human. They refused to accept limits. Although seen by conventional society as hell-raising bohemians, the Beats were seeking to rise above the restrictive materialistic mores of conventional society.

Most of the Beat Generation were homosexual or bisexual, in particular Ginsberg and Burroughs. One of the contentious issues relating to *Howl* were the lines within the text, which concerned homosexuality. *Howl* was originally written in 1955 as a performance piece. Together with Kerouac's *On the Road* and William Burroughs' *Naked Lunch*, *Howl* was considered to be the most popular and greatest works of the Beat Generation. *Howl* was published by the poet Lawrence Ferlinghetti of *City Lights Books*. However, upon its release, Ferlinghetti and bookstore manager Shigeyoshi Murao were charged with disseminating obscene literature. On October 3rd, Judge Clayton W. Horn ruled that the work was not obscene. Consequently, *Howl* went on to be revered for its hallucinatory style and frank exploration of sexuality. The prime emotional drive for the work was Ginsberg's empathy for Carl Solomon, to whom the poem was dedicated. He met Solomon in a mental institution where he was committed for ninety days.

Burroughs' *Naked Lunch* also contains highly sexual content, in particular content about homosexual practices. This work was also prosecuted for obscenity. However, victory by *Naked Lunch* and *Howl* marked the end of literary censorship in the United States. The content of Kerouac's work was also sexual; *On the Road* mentions Neal Cassady's bisexuality, likewise *Visions of Cody*; group sex was featured in *Dharma Bums*.

Why did the Beats experiment with drugs?

Drug taking was another method the Beats experimented with to achieve altered states of consciousness. They believed that drug taking enhanced creativity, insight and productivity and was a source of inspiration for the content of their writing. They used alcohol, marijuana, Benzedrine, morphine LSD and heroin and were drawn to drugs as they were drawn to jazz.

Kerouac took Benzedrine 'until he "felt he was blasting so high that he was experiencing real insights and facing real fears. With Benzedrine, he felt he was embarking on a journey of self-discovery, climbing up from one level to the next, following his insights … Benzedrine intensified his awareness and made him feel more clever"'. Indeed, it was thought that 'Each of Kerouac's books were written on something, and each of the books has some feel of what he was on most as he wrote it' (Sadie Plant, p. 114). At the beginning of the 1960s, Kerouac met Timothy Leary, an American psychologist and writer, who believed that LSD had therapeutic potential for psychiatry and was an important means to self-discovery and the expansion of the world's consciousness. He conducted experiments with LSD at Harvard University; Allen Ginsberg took part in this research, along with the writer of the influential book *One Flew over the Cuckoo's Nest*, Ken Kesey, and later Jack Kerouac and Neal Cassady. It was easy to see how Leary was an attractive person to the Beats, like them he walked his own path questioning authority and shunning conformity. Leary suggested an ideal state of being was to turn off your mind, relax and float downstream, a phrase also associated with the *Tibetan Book of the Dead* and John Lennon. Leary modelled himself on Aleister Crowley, 1875–1947, a British poet, occultist and mystic, who was a recreational drug taker. Crowley was known by the name The Great Beast 666 and like the Beats and Leary he renounced conformity, advocating the rule *Do What Thou Wilt*.

For the Beats, taking drugs was an integral part of their lifestyle; it fuelled their writing, informed the content of their fiction and developed a technique known as cut-ups.

What is the cut-up technique?

The ways in which the Beats stimulated creativity was by relinquishing control and by using chance; cut-up is a technique they used in order to achieve these goals, in particular Burroughs who struggled with his various addictions and disjointed mental state which can be argued resulted in the literary technique cut-ups.

Cut-up was a concept first used in the 1920s by the Dadaist, Tristan Tzara; he created a poem by pulling random words out of a hat. This technique was popularized by William Burroughs in the late 1950s and 1960s. He cited T. S. Eliot's definitive modernist text *The Wasteland* (1922) as one that he used to create *new* texts. Firstly, the Beats took finished, linear texts, which were cut into pieces with lines of text or single words. The pieces were then rearranged to form a *new*, non-linear text. In addition to writers, a number of musicians have used the cut-up technique to create lyrics. These include David Bowie, a musician who embraced William Burroughs' cut-up technique when writing lyrics for his songs, in particular those on the *Diamond Dogs* album; other musicians who have used the cut-up technique include Kurt Cobain, the Rolling Stones and Radiohead.

Experiment with this: Learning to Use Cut-ups

Take any linear text you have written and a feature from a newspaper. Cut both texts into lines and single words. Rearrange the pieces of text to create a non-linear text and to form new phrases and new meanings.

How was the Beats works affected by drug use?

Depending on the drugs the Beats had taken, their work was undoubtedly affected, both in terms of content and form. Under various drugs it was difficult to sustain thoughts. The mind jumped all over the place. There was a loss of control. As Sadie Plant writs in *Writing on Drugs*: 'The words run fast and loose, the thoughts can't be contained, the ideas dissipate. Characters and authors lose their plots. Words break down … notes trip each other up' (Sadie Plant, p. 133).

Experiment with this: Learning to Lose Control

Imagine a writer is working under the influence of drugs. Write a passage from a novel the writer writes, about a writer who is writing under the influence of drugs. Don't censor thoughts. Start with an idea and permit it to dissipate. Let the words come fast and freely. Allow characters and authors to lose their plots.

On the Road

This chapter explores *On the Road* in terms of form and content, with the intention of showing contemporary readers how to experiment with Jack Kerouac's techniques, in order to enhance their own writing practice. In addition, it investigates why it was the definitive text of the Beat Generation and why it is still revered and read by many people in the twenty-first century.

Why was it written?

In the writing of *On the Road*, Jack Kerouac was hitting back at conventional society and conventional writing in an attempt to establish new ground on which writing could exist and be discussed.

The chaos of war, the resulting materialistic society and the death of his brother and father had left Kerouac dislocated and with a great sense of loss. And so, when he wrote in his journal about an idea to write a book set on the road, it was 'like a message from God giving sure direction' (p. 7). He wanted to experience freedom, adventure and the joy of being alive. He wanted to express the wild side of himself before it was too late. And there was a need to escape. He felt he had burnt all his bridges. Following the arrest of his friends in a drugs raid at Ginsberg's apartment, he feared he might be questioned too. And so he had reached a turning point in his life. Kerouac was also at a point where he wanted to investigate his identity and gain a better understanding of himself, both as an American and a French Canadian. He was born Jean-Louis Lebris de Kerouac of French-Canadian parents who had immigrated to New England. He grew up speaking joual, a French–Canadian working-class dialect. He did not speak English until he was six years old. Kerouac's immigrant family history led him to question his identity and to believe that he was not a traditional middle-class American, nor was he a man of colour; he was a white outsider. He was also part of a continent filled with people of various ethnicities and backgrounds. Many of these individuals were migrating from place to place, as seasonal workers or as hobos, meeting others and having a multiplicity of encounters with them, including those of a sexual nature. *On the Road*, therefore, was written for a variety of reasons, but one of these reasons was an endeavour to define America in the face of a capitalist society fearful of threats from opposing ideologies and from people outside American borders. In addition, the novel was written in an attempt to explore *Americans*, in terms of class, ethnicity and sexuality, in particular those considered to be outside the mainstream. It was also imperative for Kerouac to find his own voice through his writing, one which expressed his identity and those for whom he felt empathy. He also wanted to experiment with literary styles, techniques and voices in an attempt to break free from the restrictions of the European literary tradition.

What did he want to achieve?

Kerouac wanted to surpass the limitations of conventional narrative. He was searching for a freedom of expression, a confessional writing style, like he was telling the story to a friend to share his adventures and to express a joy of pure being. It was his intention to turn his thinking into prose narrative, not a novel, to create a text in which he fused what he remembered with what he made up to explore the relationship between fiction and truth, incorporating images from his travels. It was not so much the *actual* words that he was concerned with, but more the rush of what was being said, the energy and passion and truth as he saw it. Although *On the Road* may be considered to be raw and lacking polish and craft, incoherent even, this was the reaction to his work he was seeking. It was this rawness that made the writing honest and evoked the melancholy music of the night and all the joy, pain, beauty, suffering and sadness of life.

And so, Kerouac set out to write a text that was against self-censorship, Cold War politics and materialism and to write one that was an outer and an inner journey, using instinct and immediacy, one in which the world might appear transformed.

What was his inspiration?

A main source of inspiration for Kerouac's *On the Road* was his relationships with the Beats, but mostly it was Neal Cassady who came into the Beat scene in 1947. The Beats were captivated by this wild man who engaged in promiscuous sex and had a frenetic lifestyle. Indeed, Ginsberg had an affair with him and became his writing tutor. Kerouac identified with Cassady as someone who was also an outsider. And also, by Kerouac's own admission, Cassady captured his interest in the same way that his brother Gerald had; they had fun together and both shared a Catholic upbringing.

It was significant that Kerouac met Cassady, four years his junior, someone who represented youth and a reaffirmation of vitality at a key point in his life, one that marked the death of his father, the annulment of his first marriage and the end of a period of hospitalization for thrombophlebitis:

> I first met Neal not long after my father died … I had just gotten over a serious illness that I won't bother to talk about except that it really had something to do with my father's death and my awful feeling that everything was dead. With the coming of Neal there really began for me that part of my life that you could call my life on the road … (p. 1)

And so, Kerouac's life changed and the narrative began, with alter egos Sal Paradise and Dean Moriarity's taking road trips and having adventures across the United States and Mexico. This was living life to the full, seeking out experience, the lifestyle Kerouac craved, but by the end of the book, Moriarity abandons Paradise along the road, because he couldn't stop and had to keep moving and because they are searching for something they do not really find.

In addition to his relationship with The Beats, *On the Road* was inspired by the network of interstate highways. It was possible to drive from New York to LA on six tanks of cheap fuel. The endless big-sky landscapes, therefore, were a metaphor for the limitless physical and interior journeys that form the basis for *On the Road*.

What was the writing style?

The style was said to be hugely influenced by Kerouac's hero James Joyce, in particular his work *Ulysses* and also by Neal Cassady's letters. Although Cassady didn't write much prose, Kerouac was impressed with the free-flowing style of his letters; he cited these as an influence on his invention of the spontaneous prose, a literary style akin to the stream of consciousness that he used in his works. Kerouac's philosophy was not to revise the work but to go with the flow of consciousness on the page, to write in a burst, writing that was emotional, spontaneous, stream of consciousness, fuelled by immediacy and improvisational techniques. In *Belief and Technique for Modern Prose*, Kerouac listed thirty *essentials* of writing spontaneous prose; some of these were *Scribbled secret notebooks and wild typewritten pages for your own joy; Submissive to everything, open, listening; In trance fixation dreaming upon object before you; Something that you feel will find its own form; Telling the true story of the world in interior monologue; Write for the world to read and see your exact picture of it; Work from pithy middle eye out, swimming in language sea ...*

Experiment with this: Learning to Write Spontaneous Prose

Take this *essential* for writing spontaneous prose and use it as a source of inspiration for a writing burst: *Write for the world to read and see your exact picture of it*. Ensure the writing is written with a sense of immediacy and use an emotional tone.

How did jazz inspire Kerouac's writing?

Alongside spontaneous prose, Kerouac also employed techniques from jazz playing, that is the use of the breath. In the sense of a musician drawing breath and blowing his saxophone until he had run out of breath and therefore his music, Kerouac used this same technique when writing. He wrote a burst of writing until he had said all that he wanted to express. Connected with the breath was the use of a long connecting dash, so that the phrases occurring between dashes might also resemble jazz licks, so that when spoken the words take on an unpremeditated rhythm. In addition, *On the Road* was written in a style that sounded like Kerouac was talking to himself. Sentences did not always come to fruition; there were interruptions, exaggerations, overloads of detail. The work had a tone of self-reminiscence and a surreal quality, an out-of-touch with reality feel, one that was mixed up and lacked a chronological order and precision, an innovative style built upon *new* techniques, a work very unlike that of the European novel.

Experiment with this: Learning to Use a *Rush* Writing Style

Imagine you are a young American writer from the 1950s, one whose ideals reflect these themes: anti-materialism, anti-establishment, soul searching and rebellion. You are living a bohemian, nomadic lifestyle. Using an American voice, write the story of one day in your life as if you are telling it to a friend in a rush, imbue the language with energy and passion. Write sentences that do not always come to fruition. Use interruptions, exaggerate and overload detail.

Although it was claimed that Kerouac did not revise his work, it became apparent that there were several drafts of the novel. His Columbia mentor Mark Van Doren claimed that Jack had outlined much of the work in notebooks over a number of preceding years. Likewise, Joyce Johnson, former girlfriend of Jack Kerouac and author of *In the Night Cafe, Come and Join the Dance, Bad Connections* and *Minor Characters* (the widely acclaimed autobiographical account of her love affair with Kerouac), also claims that he spent years revising his work and carefully crafting each paragraph.

However, for some time, Kerouac had difficulty engaging a publisher for his work due to the experimental writing style and its sympathetic tone towards marginalized groups of America and for its graphic descriptions of homosexual behaviour and drug use. The text went through a number of changes, that is the removal of many of the more sexually explicit scenes, fearing libel suits before it was finally published in 1957.

What was the experimental writing technique used in *On the Road*?

Besides stream of consciousness and techniques borrowed from jazz, Kerouac employed a technique he referred to as sketching that changed the traditional narrative form. He first used this technique in his journals. Kerouac likened sketching to that of being an artist who observed everything he saw in the street and sketched it in his notebook. The writer was the same as an artist, except that the writer sketched what he saw, whilst the writer used words. Sketching was done rapidly, almost manically, in a kind of trance, but with intensity of feeling.

Experiment with this: Learning to Use a Sketching Writing Style

Take a notepad for a walk. Find a bench in a street or park to sit on or go to a busy cafe. Drift into your own world. Like an artist sketching what they observe, you do the same; only use words instead of pencil lines. Sketch quickly what you see.

How was *On the Road* written?

Apparently, high on Benzedrine, Kerouac typed rapidly, as fast as he could, in a rush, on a continuous one hundred and twenty foot scroll of paper to avoid breaking his chain of thoughts at the end of the sheets of paper, a scroll that he cut to size and taped together. The scroll, a 125,000-word version, was typed single-spaced, without margins or paragraphs, over a three-week period in an apartment in New York's Chelsea, and when rolled out it looked like a road.

What was the form?

The scroll manuscript has been described as a 'nonfictional hybrid, equal parts diary entry and autobiography' (p. 95, in the Introduction to *On The Road* by Joshua Kupetz), also a 'circle of despair'. According to Kerouac, the circle of despair represents a belief that 'the experience of life is a regular series of deflections' from one's goals. As one is deflected from a goal, Kerouac explains, '(s)he establishes a new goal from which (s)he will inevitably also be deflected' (p. 89). And so, if a reader approaches Kerouac's sprawling prose and allows the narrative to turn, reverse, to be set back upon itself in a series of deflections and accepts that the shifting horizon of signification is part of the experience of meaning, the reader can proceed and be 'headed there at last' (p. 91). Kerouac's work then engaged the reader 'in the process of meaning by encountering unfamiliar structures' (p. 91). The sprawling poetic narrative undermined literary conventions; it was non-linear, discontinuous and did not uphold causal relationships between events, as is the case with the traditional linear plot.

What did the book capture?

With the publication of *On the Road*, the *New York Times* proclaimed that Kerouac was the voice of a new generation of American writers.

And so by capturing the spirit and events of the time in an experimental innovative writing style, one that communicated directly, honestly and emotionally and collapsed the division between life and art, *On the Road* became defined as being the definitive text of the post-Second World War Beat Generation.

On the Road also captured Kerouac's personal journey, his sense of alienation, of being adrift from middle-class America. He considered himself *different* and experienced a feeling of homelessness, of being adrift. 'I was just somebody else, some stranger, and my whole life was a haunted life, the life of a ghost' (p. 58). He considered himself to be a white man who was disillusioned with the world. He secretly wished he was a Negro. He empathized with the oppressed minorities, thinking they had more joy and darkness from their music and their lives. As Sal and Dean drove to Mexico City, the 'Fellahin Indians of the world' stare at the 'ostensibly self-important moneybag Americans on a lark in their land' (p. 59).

Following the success of *On the Road*, Kerouac became uncomfortable with his new celebrity status. His work was chosen by the *Time* magazine as one of the best English-language novels from 1923 to 2005. Following the text's success, publishers were keen for a sequel. In response, Kerouac fictionalized his adventures with Gary Snyder and other San Francisco poets, together with his experience of Buddhism, in *Dharma Bums*, published in 1958.

In the *Cult of Unthink* published in Horizon, 1958, Robert Brustein associated the Beats with the fans of JD and MB, saying that like the movie stars' fans, they were violent at the least provocation. Kerouac replied to Brustein a week before publication saying that he was not depicting violence; *On the Road* was about tenderness among wild young hell raisers like the generation of Brustein's grandfather. Kerouac was deeply hurt that anyone could consider that he exalted violence. And so began the torment of Kerouac's success. He drank more and more heavily, as he felt that *On the Road* was being misinterpreted; it was being revered by some as capturing the lives of a hip generation and criticized by others who felt it captured the lives of sordid, immoral bohemians, neither truly acknowledging the genuine seriousness of his spiritual intent.

And yet *On the Road* is still read by many, especially college students, although its influence has been wide and far-reaching. The British writer Geoff Dyer says, 'I actually find myself more vulnerable to its power as I get older. The yearning of the book, the way it burns with Kerouac's desire to write a great novel and with the consciousness that he's achieving it, is there on every page'. Singer-songwriter Tom Waits enthuses too, 'I will always owe a debt to (him) for finally opening my eyes and making me feel like it's alright to sleep 'til four in the afternoon and go out all night and take a good hard look at the underbelly of the bowels of a major urban centre'. The actor Johnny Depp speaks of the novel as being 'life changing'. Whilst photographer and artist Tom Hunter agrees, saying that when he read it, it 'changed my life', encouraging him to give up his job and *go on the road*, hitchhiking to France, meeting travellers. 'I don't think I could have done any of those things without reading *On the Road*, abandoning and rejecting everything and seeing for myself what freedom really means'. Beat biographer Bill Morgan concludes that Kerouac influenced many writers that came after him, writers who had previously been creating fiction with a beginning, middle and end began to experiment with their work. As Morgan says, people don't read *On the Road* for the plot, they 'read it for the beauty of the writing, not for the "whodunit" or the twist at the end' (*The Observer*, Mark Ellen, Research: Gemma Kappala-Ramsamy and Kit Buchan, 7 October 2012).

In addition, *On the Road* inspired the work of a number of writers who were propelled to adopt a self-conscious, frenetic, playful and sometimes ironic voice to create texts that were satirical in tone, for example, author of *One Flew over the Cuckoo's Nest* Ken Kesey and the American writer and author of *Slaughterhouse-Five* Kurt Vonnegut, not forgetting the American writer Thomas Pynchon and his work *Gravity's Rainbow* (1973), a postmodern fiction which blurs the boundaries between high and low culture and for which he shared the US National Book Award for Fiction with *A Crown of Feathers & Other Stories* by

Isaac Bashevis Singel. The journalist and author Hunter S. Thompson was also influenced by *On the Road*. Thompson became internationally known with the publication of *The Strange and Terrible Saga of the Outlaw Motorcycle Gangs* (1967) for which he spent a year living and riding with the Hells Angels. With the publication of *The Kentucky Derby Is Decadent and Depraved* (1970), he became a counter-culture figure with his *new* brand of journalism, Gonzo, an experimental style, in which the reporters involve themselves in the action and become protagonists of their stories via a first-person narrative.

Experiment with this: Learning to Experiment with Voice

Firstly, research the novels of the above writers. Make notes in response to these questions:

> What language does the author use to create these voices?
> Are certain phrases repeated?
> What is the intonation of the voice?
> Are there gaps in the text?
> How is the text phrased?
> How does each writer convey satire through the use of voice?
> Is the text fragmented?

Now, imagine a character with a self-conscious, frenetic but playful voice. Using the theme of war or mental illness, write a short novel extract in which your character reflects upon your chosen theme.

Experiment with this: Learning to Use Gonzo Journalism

Using a first-person point of view, create a reporter who tells the story of a bank robbery; the reporter becomes so involved in the action that they become a key player within the story.

Further Reading

Burroughs, S. William (1971) The Wild Boys, New York: Grove Press.

—— (2008) Junky, London: Penguin Classic.

—— (2010) Naked Lunch, London: Fourth Estate.

Cassady, Neal (1971) The First Third, San Francisco, CA: City Lights.

Dilwali, Ashok (2007) Sayings from The Upanishads, New Delhi: Niyogi Books.

Hess, Hermann (1965) Steppenwolf, London: Penguin Books.

—— (1998) Siddhartha, London: Picador.

—— (2000) The Glass Bead Game, London: Vintage.

Huxley, Aldous (2007) Brave New World, London: Vintage Classics.

—— (2011) The Doors of Perception, London: Thinking Ink Media.

Johnson, Joyce (1990) In the Night Cafe, London: Fontana.

Kerouac, Jack (1994) Doctor Sax, London: Grove Press.

—— (1995) Book of Blues, London: Penguin Classics New Edition.

—— (2000) Dharma Bums, London: Penguin Classics New Edition.

—— (2001) Visions of Cody, London: Flamingo New Edition.

—— (2007) On The Road, London: Penguin Classics New Edition.

Lachman, Gary Valentine (2001) Turn Off Your Mind, London: Sidgwick & Jackson.

Lal, P. (1994) The Bhagavad Gita, New Delhi: Roli Books.

Paramananda (2001) A Deeper Beauty, Birmingham: Windhorse Publications.

Plant, Sadie (1999) Writing on Drugs, London: Faber & Faber.

Rinpoche, Sogyal (1992) The Tibetan Book of Living & Dying, London: Ryder.

Trainor, Kevin (2001) Buddhism, London: Duncan Baird Publishers.

Section Three

When Is/Was the Postmodern Era?

It has been argued by an authority of postmodern art and architecture, Charles Jencks, that since the mid-twentieth century, in particular the early 1960s, the term 'postmodern' was used in connection with literature, economics, art and religion. Since the 1970s, however, the term 'postmodern' was embraced by academia too. So, what is it?

What is/was postmodernity?

Postmodernity is a complex multi-layered concept which describes the West's political, sociological, economic and cultural condition; it is concerned with the collapse of Soviet communism and the restructuring of capitalist society which has resulted in an increasingly post-industrial, information, service-orientated age, one where new forms of communication technology have altered the routines and relationships of everyday lives.

The very shape of existence to which we have been accustomed since the Industrial Revolution has changed dramatically. In rich countries across the globe, the old ways of measuring time are disappearing. Instant communication breaks down even further the barriers of time and space. The advent of cultural technology, the development of computer mediation, the impact of TV and the media, and the advancement of 'modern' transport and communication technologies can be seen as being significant changes in communication, for example, email, voice mail and texts. Undoubtedly the boundaries of time and space have been dramatically challenged by the electronic revolution. In addition, the linear narrative of work has been eroded; more and more people work on short-term contracts, some spending much of their time in front of screens, working, socializing, shopping, indeed, living in virtual communities. So it can be seen that postmodernity illustrates a major transition in human history. A new type of society has emerged, one that is structured around consumers and consumption, as opposed to one structured around workers and production.

Postmodernity also represents a time when there is a decline in faith, in the keystones of the Enlightenment, that is, the Grand Narratives or ideologies that control individuals and society – science, religion, history – and there is suspicion of any attempts to offer 'truths'. Some may see this as being freed from the 'old restrictions', whereas others may see it as being removed from security and hurled into a melting pot of disorientating plurality. With so many 'new truths' at our disposal, it has led us to revise our concept of truth, so that truth is believed to be something that is considered to be constructed rather than discovered. In addition, as a result of the paradigm shift brought about by social, technological and cultural change, the once universal assumptions about what constitutes the real has also been revised. So, there now exists a much more fluid and multiple sense of reality. Postmodernity, therefore, is the result of a crisis in representation and a shift in what constitutes reality and truth.

The essence, therefore, of postmodernity is that there is no essence. Instead, society moves through a world of signs, a world where everything has been done before, and all that remains is a cultural wreckage waiting to be re-worked and combined in new ways. Postmodernity then, the condition or time in which we find/found ourselves living, is/was 'a great, confusing, stressful and enormously promising historical transition, and it has to do with change not so much *what* we believe as in *how* we believe'; or more importantly, it can be said to be 'a word of looking back' at a world that has 'just now ceased to be' (Ed. Walter Truitt Anderson, Fontana Postmodernism Reader: London, 1996, pp. 2–3).

What is/was postmodernism?

'The term gets everywhere, but no one can quite explain what it is'. However, 'postmodernism' is a term that is 'ubiquitous and yet highly contradictory' (Woods, Tim, Beginning Postmodernism, Manchester University Press, pp. 1–2).

Postmodernism represents the various schools or artistic, cultural movements that have come out of the postmodern period. Through the 1980s and 1990s more people became familiar with postmodernism, either through academia or through arts, in particular literature; concrete examples of such works will be explored in this section for the benefit of readers and writers of experimental fiction. The mood of postmodernity, which challenged the Grand Narratives, has been the impetus for challenging writing practice, as will be shown, but what is postmodernism's relationship to modernism?

What is postmodernism's relationship to modernism?

In her works *A Poetics of Postmodernism* (1988) and *The Politics of Postmodernism* (1989), Linda Hutcheon has argued that modernism 'literally and physically haunts postmodernism and their interrelations should not be ignored' (Hutcheon, 1989, p. 49). There are two schools of thought about the nature and interaction of modernism and postmodernism. The first sees 'postmodernism as an extension and intensification of certain characteristics of modernism' (Hutcheon, 1989, p. 50). However, the second school sees postmodern as breaking with modernism, which can best be observed through the debate between the French philosopher, sociologist and literary theorist Jean-Francois Lyotard and the German sociologist and philosopher Jurgen Habermas.

Lyotard versus Habermas

Jean-Francois Lyotard rejects all proof or truth claims and attacks meta-narratives, the Grand Narratives or ideologies that control individuals and society. Meta-narratives, so Lyotard argues, are no longer tenable, just as there can be no moral absolutes. For Lyotard all explanations and system are narratives, as are all discourses. Religion, politics and science all produce meanings which can have no absolute truth. Lyotard argues that the criteria regulating the truth claims of knowledge derive from context-dependent 'language games'. For example, the great world religions simply tell narratives about the world and our place within it. Religion is contested and seen as an incommensurate way of knowing, with truth forever shifting. In addition to religion, science is also contested.

A major concern of Lyotard's is the different procedures and effects marking scientific and narrative knowledge. In its 'modern' phase, Lyotard claims, science sought legitimization from either of two narrative types. They were the revolutionary tradition, the prospective unity of all knowledge associated with Hegelianism, and the narrative of human liberation associated with the Enlightenment. Neither of these 'meta-narratives', argues Lyotard, now has credibility. Instead, 'postmodern' science pursues the technical and commercial aims of optimal performance, a change reinforced by new computerized technologies which make information a political quantity. Computers, then, guarantee scientific legitimization because they have shifted the emphasis from intrinsic values to performativity.

In 1980, Jurgen Habermas entered the postmodernism debate with his essay *Modernity versus Postmodernity*. He disagreed with Lyotard, arguing that various postmodern theories are an attack on modernity itself. Habermas argues that 'postmodernism is no different from modernism in certain formal respects'. Indeed, 'Postmodernism is a *knowing* modernism, a *self-reflexive* modernism'. In other words,

Postmodernism does what modernism does, only in a celebratory rather than repentant way. Thus, instead of lamenting the loss of the past, the fragmentation of existence and the collapse of selfhood, postmodernism embraces these characteristics as a new form of social existence and behaviour. The difference between modernism and postmodernism is therefore, best seen as a difference in *mood* or *attitude*, rather than a chronological difference, or a different set of aesthetic practices. (Woods Tim, Beginning Postmodernism, pp. 8–9)

So, what has postmodernism got to do with fiction?

What has postmodernism got to do with fiction?

A postmodern artist or writer is in the position of a philosopher: the text he writes, the work he produces are not in principle governed by pre-established rules, and they cannot be judged according to a determined judgement, by applying familiar categories to the text or the work. Those rules and categories are what the work of art is looking for. The arts and the writer, then, are working without rules in order to formulate the rules of what will have been done (Jean-Francois Lyotard, *The Postmodern Condition: A Report on Knowledge*, Manchester: Manchester University Press, 1984, p. 81).

Postmodern fiction can be said to be a response to the changes and uncertainty as a result of twentieth-century questions relating to the world and an individual's place in it; therefore, it is fiction that challenges the traditional notion of a world which is logical, coherent and ordered and portrays a world that is elusive, baffling and in a state of flux. The fiction borne out of this period, which will be explored in this section, endeavours to address the crisis in representations, including questioning the nature of language; it also investigates multiple realities, multiple selves, whilst interrogating the realist version of fixed meanings.

Postmodern writers are not homogeneous in their work. However, amongst the multiplicity of narratives used by them, there is a common objective, that is, to challenge the psychological realism central to realist fiction.

Postmodern fiction challenges the very idea of any meaning being fixed and stable through the use of textual gaps. Within realist fiction, there is an unproblematic relationship between the actual word and what the word evokes; this is in stark contrast to postmodern works, where there is no correspondence between the signifier and the signified. In 1916, the Swiss linguist Ferdinand de Saussure claims that language is a system consisting of arbitrary signs, in which there is no direct link between the sign and the concept it evokes. However, in the twentieth century, fiction is dominated by the gap between these signifiers and what they signify or represent. In other words, the emphasis is placed on the signifier rather than the signified; this, therefore, has the effect of making postmodern fiction more interactive than realist fiction, it challenges the reader to create the work's meaning by filling in the gaps. In Jon McGregor's collection of short stories *This Isn't The Sort of Thing That Happens to Someone Like You*, set mostly around the fenland landscape, what is withheld is as important to the reader as what is revealed, for it is for the reader to deduce what is withheld. In *The Winter Sky*, for example, there is a linear narrative on one page and on the opposite page there is what Joanna 'wrote about the boy in her notebook' (p. 6).

> In summer the sky is blue & lifted high
>   a shimmering blue silence from which
>   there is no hiding place
>   (save) beneath the surface of the land. (p. 7)

The reader is constantly left guessing and is required to fill in the gaps. In addition, the postmodern writer plays with the reader's expectations, uses juxtaposition and subverts stereotypes, rendering the work with a sense of playfulness or 'jouissance' as Barthes describes, encouraging the reader to interact with, and interpret, the work. McGregor's short story *Fleeing Complexity* simply reads: 'The Fire spread quicker than the little bastard was expecting' (p. 75).

What are postmodern writing strategies and techniques?

Although, on the one hand, postmodernism can be said to be elitist, exclusive and academic, on the other, it can be liberating and can inspire *new* writing practice, one that employs a variety of writing strategies and techniques, which will be investigated later in this section for the benefit of readers of experimental fiction, and writers wishing to experiment in order to create new works of their own.

Postmodernism resists all notions of continuity; therefore, fiction is fragmented, dislocated, abstract and sometimes it is simply a kaleidoscope of impressions. Work, therefore, often takes the form of short, fragmented sections, which can, and often do, develop into self-contained narratives, which are often disparate in terms of content; the textual gaps between sections frequently experiment with typographical devices; for example, in his work *Generation X*, the Canadian-born writer Douglas Coupland uses cartoon-style illustrations and slogans to create gaps within the narrative, for example: 'ECONOMY OF CHOICE IS RUINING CHOICE' (p. 89).

Fiction is playful, ironic and engages with the past; it is concerned with bricolage, assembling something new out of existing texts, that is, fairy tales, myths and folk legends. In her collection of short stories, *The Bloody Chamber*, the late British writer Angela Carter rewrites fairy tales to address feminist issues. She plays with women's roles and their sexuality by challenging the way women are portrayed; for example, *The Bloody Chamber* is a re-telling of *Bluebeard*, but instead of the heroine being rescued by a male hero, she's rescued by her mother.

Some postmodern work employs frequent time shifts; this is apparent in *Slaughterhouse-Five* by Kurt Vonnegut. Vonnegut was born in 1922 in Indianapolis. During the Second World War he served in Europe; as a prisoner of war in Germany, he witnessed the destruction of Dresden, an experience which inspired *Slaughterhouse-Five* and the time-traveller, prisoner of war, protagonist, Billy Pilgrim:

> 'Listen:
>
> Billy Pilgrim has come unstuck in time.
>
> Billy has gone to sleep a senile widower and awakened on his wedding day. He has walked through a door in 1955 and come out another one in 1941. He has gone back through that door to find himself in 1963. He has seen his birth and death many times,' he says, and pays random visits to all the events in between'. (p. 17)

To believe Barthes, a text is simply 'a multi-dimensional space in which a variety of writings, none of them original, blend and clash. The text is a tissue of quotations drawn from the innumerable centres of culture' (*Death of the Author*). Postmodern writers then are at liberty to experiment with their fiction by mixing old and new cultural forms, fact and fiction, different genres. They raid high and popular culture for signs and images, and representations of mass media and consumer commodities, which in turn are incorporated into their literary works, as Coupland writes in Generation X: 'SEMI-DISPOSABLE SWEDISH FURNITURE' (p. 84), 'Japanese Minimalism' (p. 85).

Indeed, postmodern writers recycle narratives, enjoying the practice of intertextuality, referencing other texts, in order to generate novelty and creativity. There is emancipation in being able to poach other discourses in order to tell stories, stories which rewrite the narratives of history and science allowing the reader to see the world with fresh eyes; stories which celebrate linguistic play and invention; stories which investigate our many worlds and selves, and in so doing, writers celebrate difference, and delight in uncertainty and collapse of meaning, allowing readers to escape from the claustrophobia of fixed belief systems so that they can bring their own multiple meanings to the work. As a result of the old truths being broken down, writers are free to rewrite them anew.

Postmodern fiction refuses unity; it actively engages with the moving play of signifiers rather than attempting to constrain plurality as in traditional realist fiction. Pluralism is the focus of postmodernism, and there is an underlying dismissal of the concept of a coherent self. Postmodern fiction vehemently rejects a single centre of consciousness and is replaced by a series of simultaneous, overlapping narratives which continually defer resolution. As the British writer Jeanette Winterson says in *Art Objects*: ' ... I am a writer who does not use plot as an engine or foundation. What I do use are stories within stories within stories' (p. 189). Therefore, meaning is never fixed or single; it is constantly shifting, opening up endless possibilities for the reader and writer. Complete meaning escapes; there are flickerings or scatterings of meaning; meaning is transient, incomplete, uncertain, reflecting the chaotic, messy, shifting world it reflects, and is born out of. Winterson would agree: 'For me, the fragments of the image I seek are stellar; they beguile me as stars do, I seek to describe them, to interpret them, but I cannot possess them, they are too far away' (p. 169). Postmodern fiction, then, is fiction sometimes composed from fragmented images; these images can often be so fragmented that the work is rendered ambiguous and difficult to read. However, 'Readers who don't like books that are not printed television, fast on thrills and feeling, soft on the brain, are not critising literature, they are missing it altogether' (p. 35). Therefore, it is up to the reader to become actively engaged with the text to bring about their own meaning. As Barthes says in *Death of the Author*: 'A text is made of multiple writings drawn from many cultures and entering into mutual relations of dialogue, parody, contestation, but there is one place where this multiplicity is focused and that place is the reader, not, as was hitherto said, the author.'

Postmodern fiction, therefore, experiments with form and language and can be seen as an attack on traditional realist works and an abandonment of the traditional linear plot. Postmodern fiction relies on mood rather than plot, indeed a 'variety of mood and tone to make way for those intenser moments when the writer and the word are working at maximum tautness' (Winterson, Art Objects, p. 173). There is an attitude that pervades in postmodern fiction which suggests that realist fiction has lost all credibility. The idea behind the work of a number of postmodern writers is that the conventions of realism are exhausted; it is therefore impossible to create an original literary work and themes reflect this 'end' of writing. So, out of this environment, a new fiction emerges: metafiction. Metafiction is preoccupied with its own construct and status, it exposes the craft of the text, drawing attention to the text's factiousness, resulting in self-reflexive, self-conscious fiction, as Dennis Potter writes in his novel *Hide and Seek*:

> "He knows I am trying to escape", announced Daniel Miller, abruptly.
> "Who does? Who knows?"
> "The Author". (p. 1)

Therefore, postmodern writers are free to create narratives which question fiction, exposing fiction as fiction, questioning fiction's own relation to the real. Postmodern writers create narratives which ask such questions as: what is a writer, a reader, a narrative?

What are the similarities and differences between postmodern and modern fiction?

There are many similarities between the modern and the postmodern; both movements are concerned with experimentation and fragmentation and both question what constitutes reality. And yet, there are also differences; for example, modernism is exempt from the implication in popular culture; it partly defines itself by separation from the popular, unlike postmodernism, which relishes popular and consumer culture and celebrates it, which can be best illustrated in the fiction of Douglas Coupland and the American writers Brett Easton Ellis and Don DeLillo, fiction that will be explored later in this section.

For the postmodern writer, fragmentation is playful and a celebration of the liberation from fixed truths and beliefs; they delight in difference and uncertainty and revel in playfully mixing 'high' with 'popular' cultural forms, the material and the spiritual, tradition and the new, to generate novelty and creativity. In addition, postmodern writers recycle narratives, genres and discourses, in an eclectic fashion, so that there appears to be nothing more than surface, no depth, no significance. This celebration of flexibility, play and self-reflexivity is a central element of postmodern fiction.

The modern writer, by contrast, laments fragmentation, seeing it as symptomatic of a systematic collapse of meaning and value. Modern is also exempt from the implication in popular culture; instead, it partly defines itself by its separation from the popular. Modern fiction strove for an accepted, albeit elusive truth, whereas postmodern fiction questions the possibility of saying something truthful in a world where there is no longer an agreement on what truth or reality is. In *Postmodernist Fiction* (1987), Brian McHale considers modernism to be dominated by epistemological questions, that is, modernism questioned ways in which reality can be known. Fiction foregrounds questions such as: How can I interpret this world of which I am a part? And what am I in it? Other questions include, What is there to be known? Who knows it? How do they know it, and with what degree of certainty? McHale speaks of modern, epistemological devices: 'the multi-implication and juxtaposition of perspectives', and of the existence of a 'single centre of consciousness' (McHale, 1987, p. 9).

Postmodernism, however, is dominated by ontological questions, that is, postmodernism questions whether reality is knowable at all (McHale, p. 9). There are 'multi-implication and juxtaposition of perspectives' but there is not 'a single centre of consciousness'.

However, as Tim Woods says, 'Modernism tore up unity and postmodernism has been enjoying the shreds' (Woods, 1999, p. 8). This implies that postmodernism is a sophisticated modernism, one that is no longer characterized by angst, seeing change as a nightmare, quite the reverse to postmodern, which sees change as inevitable; this can be displayed in the work of the British Indian novelist Salman Rushdie, to be investigated in this section too.

And so, postmodernism does what modernism does, but in a celebratory manner, rather than a nostalgic, pessimistic one. Modernism's multiplication of perspectives can be seen as leading to postmodernism's dispersion of voices, and modernism's collage can be seen as leading to postmodernism's self-conscious genre-splicing and mixing. In addition, the deconstruction of signs and their reconstruction allows the modern writer to create new meaning through juxtaposition. In contrast, postmodern fiction, by its very practice of playful fragmentation and intertextuality, collapses all meaning.

What does postmodern fiction represent?

Postmodern fiction is fiction which represents an immense power of ideas and can promote a whole new way of thinking about language, representation and communication. It is a fiction which goes beyond contemporary reality, rejecting the boundaries of time and space, science and mythology, therefore creating new fictions to reflect the new world and our multiple narratives, multiple selves and multiple points of view. It is a fiction which explores debates concerning reality, science, religion, history, consumer culture, technology, representations of gender and sexuality.

Postmodern writing revives forms of writing from the past whilst experimenting with media-based forms of the future, fiction that will be explored in this section of the book, in order that readers of experimental fiction can learn about the historical era, postmodernity, and understand what postmodern writers are doing within their texts. In addition, writers of experimental fiction can become familiar with postmodern techniques and experiment with them in their own writing practice.

Identity in Flux

In order that readers of experimental fiction can comprehend what the term 'identity in flux' means, this chapter explores the *new* representations of gender, the body and sexuality in postmodern fiction; it will also outline what can be attributed to these *new* representations in literary works, works that are deemed to be experimental, in terms of both form and content. Therefore, writers of experimental fiction will be able to explore these 'new' forms and content, as well as techniques and strategies, within their own work.

What has contributed to new perceptions of gender, the body and sexuality in the postmodern era?

Even as far back as 1949, Simone de Beauvoir's *The Second Sex* claimed that gender, as distinct from biological sex, is a construct, something made by society, that is, one is not born a woman. If gender, then, is a construct and can be changed, manipulated and even performed, it can be viewed as a facet of a multiple, contradictory, fluid identity, one, that is, in flux.

Since the 1980s and 1990s, the world has become ever more complex and fluid; borders have fallen or have been crossed, access to the Internet has increased, so that individuals are learning to comprehend a multiplicity of view points and many ways of experiencing reality and identity. As Ian Gregson writes in *Postmodern Literature*, ' ... a stable sense of identity has been persistently undermined' (p. 41). It is a world where many of the old certainties, truths and beliefs have shifted, allowing individuals to experiment with their identities, sexualities and bodies. There is a plurality of opportunities to alter the body and its image: piercings, tattoos, body modification are readily available. Instead of identity being seen as something fixed and determined by social or cultural roles, it can be seen as something that can be constructed and reconstructed, leading to such questions as: What does it mean to be male? What does it mean to be female?

And so, the period of postmodernity has led to changes in the way gender, the body and sexuality have come to be perceived, with the self being viewed as a construct continually in process. Therefore, for readers and writers of experimental fiction, it is imperative to have an understanding, as to what has contributed to these changes.

Undoubtedly the rise of the Women's Movement and other movements, notably Gay Pride, questioned gender assumptions. What were once constituted as gender norms has been called into question, leading to a newly fluid and unstable view of identity; this has been key to the cultural shift which marks the postmodern, a space where different voices can be heard. Where there was once a more clear definition of gender roles and gender spaces, both roles and spaces have now become blurred. More and more men are becoming homemakers, choosing to raise children, while women are taking on the role of breadwinner; therefore, concepts of gender roles have undergone a transition. In addition, with the acceleration of developments in technology and the media, advertising stereotypes of female and male have been subverted, to fall in line with these shifts, challenging the old models of male and female norms, so that men and women often see themselves through images of consumer culture. In addition, oppressive forms of femininity and maybe to a lesser degree, masculinity, and socio-cultural definitions of desirability are no longer fixed. This has implications for the body and sexuality, including sexual practices, which in turn has impacted upon the practice of writing and reading postmodern fiction which experiments with these new representations in new ways. But how?

Why are *new* representations of gender, the body and sexuality reflected in postmodern fiction?

If writers and readers, in any era, are living through a paradigm shift, the cultural and social changes that occur become a focus of interest for a number of writers, and they experiment with these *new* representations in their work, so fiction can be seen to be consolidating this shift.

Postmodern fiction reflects postmodern identities, ones that have opened up new cultural spaces within which different forms of social and sexual relationships are happening. Fluid identity is characteristic of postmodern fiction, which, as McHale argues, raises such questions as: 'Which world is this? What is to be done in it? Which of my selves is to do it?' (McHale, 1987, p. 10). And so it appears that boundaries between male and female have blurred. Social, cultural, economic and political developments have allowed for the evolution of identity, and this is reflected in literary works.

In addition, in the postmodern world, sexuality is not fixed. The climate is one that encourages flexibility and experimentation; individuals can be gay, straight, gay again, then bisexual. As Joseph Bristow suggests:

> Bisexuality unsettles uncertainties: straight, gay, lesbian. It has affinities with all of these, and is delimited by none. It is, then, and identity, that is also not an identity, a sign of the certainty of ambiguity, the stability of instability, a category that defines and defeats categorisations. Bi thinking, then, definitely shares the postmodern emphasis on the indeterminacy of the sign. Moving across sexes, across genders, across sexualities, bi-ness warmly embraces multiple desires and identifications while repudiating all 'monosexual' imperatives.
> (Sexuality, London, Routledge, 1997, p. 225)

Postmodern fiction, which is working outside the traditional, not only seeks to reflect the changes, it also seeks to challenge beliefs and to stimulate new ways of thinking, new ways of seeing and new ways of being in the world; for example, the experimental writer Christine Brooke-Rose, in her 1968 novel *Between*, omitted the verb 'to be' to stress the narrator's disorientated sense of identity and in her 1998 fiction *Next*, she had twenty-six narrators, whose names began with a different letter of the alphabet. In this fiction, she omitted the verb 'to have' to emphasis the loss of identity the homeless Londoners experience in the book. But who else is writing about identity and how are they doing it?

Which postmodern writers have experimented with identity, the body and sexuality in their work, and how?

Kathy Acker, an American, bisexual, experimental novelist and cult figure of the punk movement, was strongly influenced by William Burroughs, Marguerite Duras, the Black Mountain School, the Fluxus Movement and literary theory, especially French feminism. She was a writer who experimented with identity, sexuality, the body, violence, desire and pleasure in her fiction, claiming her novels were also influenced by her experience as a stripper.

In her writing, Acker, in an eclectic fashion, recycles and combines plagiarism, cup-up technique, pastiche, autobiography, pornography, French feminism, philosophy and literary theory, and in so doing, she blurs the distinction between popular and high art and obliterates literary hierarchies. By embracing a multiplicity of discourses, and references to other texts, Acker destabilizes and fragments her fiction in order to portray the instability of female identity. By employing this process, she confounds expectations of what fiction can be. Also, she illustrates that

> Feminism is an essential part of postmodernism … one of the traits of postmodernism is decanonization of all master codes, all conventions, institutions, authorities. Likewise this 'decanonization is what feminism

is all about, for feminist texts deconstruct women's oppression and displace the centre of attention away from men ... feminist texts often abandon plot and causality, dislocating organization, disrupting syntax, exploiting word play and intertextuality. (Smyth, Edmund, *Postmodernism & Contemporary Fiction*, p. 156)

Experiment with this: Learning to Experiment with Identity and Sexuality Using Multiple Discourses

Write a short story by assembling a bricolage of multiple discourses, for example, literary theory, pastiche and parody; use puns and disrupt syntax too. Use this as a starting point: I became someone else for a night and a day ...

Some see Kathy Acker's work as a form to be contested because of her manipulation of texts, in which she blurs the boundaries of creativity and plagiarism; for example, in 1982, she rewrote Charles Dickens' *Great Expectations*. She also *borrowed* the work of Marcel Proust and Marquis de Sade. Some critics refer to her as a literary terrorist; others view her explicit manipulation of existing literary works as being very skilful. There is also a mixed response to the content of writing, some seeing it as exposing sexual domination as a form of oppression, others seeing it as the objectifying of women.

In her work *Don Quixote*, Don is a young woman engaging with poststructuralist theory, wandering the streets of New York and St. Petersburg having had a meltdown, following an abortion. She recognizes the world's frauds, fakes and lies and regards identity as an internalized fictional construct. *Memoriam to Identity* is steeped in French philosophy and literary theory and engages with questions of identity, violence, authorship and the body.

Experiment with this: Learning to Experiment with New Ways of Viewing the Body by Using Different Points of View

Write a section from a novel in which a character either

Celebrates one's body
Reconstructs one's body
Transcends one's body
Has one's body tattooed
Has one's body pierced

Jeanette Winterson also explores identity, the body and sexuality in her fiction; it is concerned with a collision of discourses, especially the language of fairy tales. The fact that fairy tales are rich with symbols, metaphors and binaries, and also that they are formulaic, means that Winterson is able to play with their codes and conventions. Well-known plot structures can be re-arranged. It is also possible to free characters from their traditional contexts and place them in new ones, or manipulate and challenge the boundaries of time and space; doing these things can be liberating for a writer, and fun for the reader.

Winterson produces works which are an exploration of certain postmodernist ideas through an overlapping set of narratives, stories within stories, which deny the conventional presumption of a linear form in narrative. Instead, the narratives collapse, fictively, into one another, and cross the boundaries between history and fiction, realism and fairy tale. This blending of styles and blurring of boundaries, to produce an effect of pastiche, is predominant in *Sexing the Cherry*. Winterson uses alternative authoritative narrative in *The Story of the Twelve Dancing Princesses*. A mini narrative within *Sexing the Cherry* shows a princess falling in love with a woman, not a man. Also, all the princesses within Winterson's narrative reject marriage, preferring to live in exclusively female communities, and so they eradicate their husbands. She also explores lesbian desire; one of the princesses falls in love with a woman. 'I wanted to run my finger from the cleft in her chin down the slope of her breasts and across the level plains of her stomach to where I knew she would be wet' (p. 54).

Winterson subverts patriarchal truths and explores new representations of identity within her fiction. Dog-Woman, in *Sexing the Cherry*, is a grotesque figure whose size is intimidating to men. Indeed, she bites off their penises. *Sexing the Cherry* is a novel which problematizes language in relation to identity. Winterson uses the male character, Jordan, to convey that 'Language always betrays us'. He claims that it 'tells the truth when we want to lie' (Winterson, 1989, p. 90). Jordan also articulates gender difference and how this is reflected through language. 'I noticed that women have a private language. A language not dependent on the constructions of me but structured by signs and expressions, and that uses ordinary words as code-words meaning something other' (p. 31). By referring to women's 'private language', Winterson illustrates the fact that language shifts according to situations or identities which can be assumed. Jordan discovers women's language by becoming a woman and having access to women's spaces.

Patriarchal values have been subverted within *Sexing the Cherry*. Winterson does this by rewriting old narratives and making them *new*. She rewrites fairy tales, in particular *The Twelve Dancing Princesses*. Although in the rewriting all the princesses reject marriage:

> We had been married a few years when a man came to the door selling brushes ... I asked him what he had in his other bag, the one he hadn't opened.
>
> 'What was it you wanted?' he asked.
> 'Poison ... '
> 'Yes, for the rats'.
> 'No, for my husband'. (p. 55)

Experiment with this: Learning to Rewrite Narratives

Take the narrative of Cinderella and put it into a contemporary context. Subvert Cinderella's traditional gender role: she is not passive nor is she a domestic slave, but she does have a life full of conflict; what is the conflict? How does she escape from it? Who helps her? Write the story.

In the 1990s, Chuck Palahniuk's *Fight Club* was published to great acclaim; this fiction was later made into a film. *Fight Club* addresses issues of gender identity; it explores the crisis in masculinity brought about by 'A generation of men raised by women' and the impact of consumer culture on masculinity. In addition, it serves to warn the reader of consumerism and to be mindful of constructions of gender that are prevalent in the media.

The narrator represents the American man who has been feminized and disempowered as a result of living in a consumer society. As Tyler says, 'We're designed to be hunters and we're in a society of shopping'. Through his relationship with Tyler Durden, and the creation of fight clubs, hosting bare-knuckle matches, the narrator seeks to reclaim his masculine identity. If postmodern society produces fragmented identities, violence appears in this novel as a means by which the fragmented self can experience pain, and therefore feeling which in turn makes the men masculine and truly alive. They can also reclaim their bodies, inscribing them with cuts and bruises, symbols of masculinity, their violent histories.

What makes this novel postmodern is the reality it creates inside itself, the way it questions reality, and produces two identities, two characters, two points of view, existing side by side, who in fact are the same character, Tyler and the narrator. This plays with the reader's perceptions and expectations in a dislocating and subtle manner.

Experiment with this: Learning to Play with a Reader's Perceptions

Create two characters who are actually the same character. Begin by writing: This is how I met Chuck Brown, I asked if Chuck was ... (continue writing ...)

And so it can be seen that there has been a cultural shift towards a different kind of masculinity and femininity. In some ways, this has to do with different visions, views and pleasures, but also with a cynicism that refuses to take the world too seriously and feels ironic towards previous generations. Consequently, there are a number of postmodern writers who are exploring and experimenting with *new* representations of gender, sexuality and the body within their fiction, and they are doing this in numerous ways, by employing a variety of postmodern techniques and strategies, for example, rewriting existing *old* texts, by subverting patriarchal views of gender, employing intertextuality and multiple discourses, and utilizing cut-up techniques.

The Fictiveness of Fiction

This chapter investigates how consumer culture, the media, rapid technological growth and the Information Age have influenced postmodern writers; their writing techniques will also be explored so that readers and writers of experimental fiction can use these techniques in their own writing.

What is the impact of consumer culture on postmodern fiction?

Consumer culture is one that encourages consumers to purchase services and goods in ever-increasing amounts, and without doubt, some postmodern fiction sets out to capture what it means to live through this experience. This is most apparent in the work of a group of young East Coast Americans writing during the 1980s and 1990s, writers referred to as the literary Brat Pack: Jay Mclnerney, Tama Janowitz and, perhaps most well known, Brett Easton Ellis.

What form, content, themes and writing strategies do postmodern writers employ to reflect consumer society?

The fiction of the Brat Pack is usually set in New York or Los Angeles and is saturated with references to TV programmes, song titles, designer labels, brand names of expensive cars, alcohol, drugs and references to the corporate world. The lifestyle of the characters is reduced to endless choice, fad, style, play, convenience and consumption, a lifestyle that reflects a superficial, 'all surface no depth', postmodern existence.

Ellis writes in *American Psycho*: 'I'm wearing a wing-collar jacquard waistcoat by Kilgour, French & Stanbury from Barney's, a silk bow tie from Saks, patent-leather slip-ons by Baker-Benjes, antique diamond studs from Kentshire Galleries and a gray wool silk-lined coat with drop sleeves and a button-down collar by Luciano Soprani' (p. 121). By employing these cultural signifiers, there emerges the world of the 1980s yuppie youth culture living in a consumer society, which is dehumanizing and spiritually depleting, a society where there is a sense of hopelessness and homelessness.

Themes of violence and pornography render the fiction controversial. However, these themes serve to illustrate the gluttony of commercialism where everything, including people, sex and the body, are commodities, addictively consumed to no avail, because all that the consuming creates is further desires and wants.

In Ellis' books, the characters are not necessarily distinguished from each other by the way they speak, behave and interact, which is the means by which traditional characters are differentiated; instead, they are set apart by their choice of designer clothes, and drug and alcohol preferences. And women, particularly, are viewed as empty, glamorous objects to be consumed, or they too are seen to be consuming extravagantly.

Ellis' fiction is often written in what can arguably be described as a *dazed* prose style, that is, the use of a dispassionate and disconnected voice to recount the narrative. This voice resonates aptly with the shallow consumer culture it represents. *In Less Than Zero*, the young, rich Clay describes his hedonistic experiences of drugs, violence and sex in an emotionless, stream of consciousness, present-tense voice, conveying that Clay is just a passive receptor for the action that goes on around him. The book reads less like a novel, more like an unconventional form of autobiography. Indeed, the lives of the characters, and that of the author, are inextricably linked. The atmosphere, then, is one of alienation and dislocation, despair and horror. In *Less Than Zero*, people are 'being mad by living in the city. Images of parents were so hungry and unfulfilled that they ate their own children' (end of book). In addition, anything and everyone can be abandoned, replaced or eradicated as easily as one can take a pill.

American Psycho's first chapter 'April Fools' opens with 'Abandon all hope ye who enter here'; this is 'scrawled in blood red lettering on the side of the Chemical Bank... and just as Timothy Price notices the words a bus pulls up, the advertisement for Les Miserables on its side blocking his view' (p. 1). The graphic violence to follow seems to echo the tone set by this opening. And whereas in traditional realist fiction an explanation is often given to account for the actions of the killer, this is not the case in *American Psycho*; the reader never really understands the motivations behind the crimes of the protagonist, Patrick Bateman.

There are numerous postmodern writing strategies the Brat Pack generation experiments with, for example, metafiction devices, those of disrupting the text, playing and manipulating genres by disrupting their codes and conventions. And, although the form of Ellis' work is often traditional, in terms of form and techniques, the structure of *Less Than Zero* is interesting. Whilst criticizing MTV culture as passive, Ellis uses its structure to frame the narrative.

In his 1991 novel *Generation X*, the Canadian writer Douglas Coupland investigates a generation of people in their twenties who have come of age in a technological, materialistic, bureaucratic society, one of Watergate, yuppies, recession, TV, divorce and crack; as a consequence, they are alienated, emotionally scarred and loathe to become an advertiser's target market, so they quit their dreary careers to move away from civilization, to the California desert. They have nowhere to direct their anger and their disturbing inner worlds.

There are numerous postmodern strategies that Coupland uses in *Generation X* to illustrate his satire of consumer culture; for example, as the narratives progress, they are interrupted by slogans, images, cartoons, much in the same way that advertising for consumer products frequently disrupts individuals' lives. However, these interruptions comment satirically and wittily on the consumer world inhabited by the characters: 'Bleeding Ponytail: An elderly sold-out baby boomer who pines for hippie or pre-sellout days' (p. 25). These fragmentations are mini narratives in their own right. 'Veal-fattening Pen: Small, cramped office workstations built of fabric-covered disassemblable wall partitions and inhabited by junior staff members. Named after the small preslaughter cubicles by the cattle industry' (p. 24). In addition, the narratives are littered with cultural signifiers, from high and popular art, for example, Dali clock and Bob Hope, which take the reader into other narratives. There are references to drugs, destruction of crops, keratosis lesions, liposuction fat and microwaved pizzas, which comment further on the negative force of consumer society, although, unlike Ellis, Coupland is playful and uses humour; he also has an affection for his characters.

Experiment with this: Learning to Create a Satirical Text Which Experiments with Disruption and Fragmentation

Create three disillusioned characters and three narratives in which the characters relate experiences from their lives, but use humour and disrupt the text with slogans and cartoons which address issues of eighties postmodern life. Choose from some of the following to use as slogans, mini narratives or comments, as Coupland does: I am not a consumer, Don't spend my inheritance, MTV sucks. A valium a day is the way.

What is the impact of rapid technological growth and the information age on postmodern fiction?

As the writer William Gibson says: 'Much of history has been, often to an unrecognized degree, technologically driven ... Technology has driven change' (Distrust That Particular Flavour, p. 61). This technological change has impacted on writers so hugely that new forms of fiction emerge and become present in the literary canon, in particular a *new* science fiction, otherwise known as cyberpunk.

When did cyberpunk emerge?

It emerged in the 1980s and 1990s, when writers such as William Gibson, Pat Cadigan, Bruce Sterling, Douglas Coupland, Jeff Noon and Harlan Ellison emerged as cyberpunk writers. Yet, the forerunner of this genre is Philip K. Dick, an American author of 44 novels and 100 short stories. Born in 1928, he began writing exclusively in the science fiction genre, around the time of the Second World War. The fiction of Dick anticipates the media-shaped world of simulation associated with postmodernity. Consequently, his writing has been highly influential in shaping and forming those writers who came after him.

Dick's fiction explores sociological, political and metaphysical themes in worlds controlled by authoritarian corporations and governments. He addresses issues such as paranoia and drug abuse, issues that reflect his experiences in life. In addition, his fiction experiments with time, madness, multiple realities and parallel universes. He illustrates in his work how susceptible to change reality can be and this, therefore, has implications for the concept of history. His most well-known novel *Do Androids Dream of Electric Sheep?* is set in a post-apocalyptic near future, 2021, in the San Francisco Bay Area, a place affected by radioactive dust following World War Terminus. The plot revolves around the protagonist Rick Deckard, a bounty hunter, whose task is to 'retire' six escaped Nexus-6 androids, whilst John Isidore, who has been changed by the radiation, a 'chickenhead', aids the fugitive androids. The work deals with profound philosophical questions: What is real? What is delusion? Fundamentally, the novel explores what it means to be human and what qualities separate humans from androids who have no sense of empathy. In addition, it addresses human feelings of love and isolation. The novel has been adapted into the film *Blade Runner*.

What is cyberpunk?

Computers, surveillance systems and the Internet all feature strongly in cyberpunk fiction – a fiction which is a mix of genres: the Western and Thriller, Sci Fi and Dystopian Fiction. It is the mix that makes it speak the postmodern condition so well, exploring not only capitalism, but also the decentring of the human consciousness in its innovative investigation of cyberspace.

The term 'cyberspace' was created by William Gibson, a term applied to the space generated by software within a computer that produces a Virtual Reality experience, one which convinces our senses that we are in another world. However, more generally, cyberspace is the 'nowhere space' through which we can download information and become part of an online community. Gibson's novel *Neuromancer* (1984) is seen as the definitive cyberpunk text with its decentring of the human consciousness, its exploration of cyberspace, its preoccupation with late capitalism and its mix of genres.

A novel compared with *Neuromancer* is *Vurt* by Jeff Noon. *Vurt* tells the story of Scribble and his gang, The Stash Riders, as they search for Desdemona. The novel is set in an alternative Manchester, one in which society is shaped by Vurt, a hallucinogenic drug-shared reality, accessed by sucking on colour-coded feathers. There is a re-telling of the myth, *Orpheus Visit to the Underworld*, in which *Vurt* explores what it means to be human in relation to the non-human.

What are the themes in cyberpunk fiction?

The themes that have been cited for Dick's work are the dominant ones in cyberpunk fiction, for example, conspiracy theories, notions of being under surveillance, which leads to the loss of an individual's privacy, issues of national security, debates concerning reality and the nature of information overload. The nature of time and anxieties about the past, the future and the present are also dominant themes.

What fictional techniques do cyberpunk writers utilize in their work?

Fundamentally, cyberpunk is more concerned with scientific ideas rather than plot and character; in this way it echoes the interests of other postmodern writers, in particular Jeff Noon, who has said that he is more interested in subject matter and atmosphere than he is in plot and character, and he is driven towards experimentation. His avant-gardism has never been exclusively literary. He cites music and the visual arts as central to the way in which he approaches his literary craft. In particular, it was when he was touring nightclubs with authors from the rave-scene anthology *Disco Biscuits* that he found his voice. Listening to a reader before him, while he waited for his turn to go on stage, he was aware of the techno-music pumping away in the next room, and it was overlapping the reading in a thought-provoking way. As a consequence of his disco days, Noon came up with the idea of dub, that is, early 70s reggae when the likes of the musician King Tubby would manipulate an already existing tune on the B-side of a vinyl using empty space and silence to reveal the skeleton of a tune. Noon then began to manipulate language in the same way that a musician manipulates music. He went on to develop remixing techniques, incorporating 'samples' in texts ranging from Shakespeare to racehorse names, best shown in his work: *Cobralingus*. In a sense, Noon's approach is not dissimilar to the Beats' cut-up technique.

The Scottish writer Irvine Welsh, author of *Trainspotting*, although not a cyberpunk writer, has also stated that disco culture, sampling and mixing were techniques he experimented within his fiction, especially in his collection of short stories *The Acid House*, in which he blends gritty realism with a crazy, drug-induced fantasy which impacts on the layout and typography of the texts.

There are many fictional techniques cyberpunk writers use in their work. They break down barriers between 'high' and 'low', relishing the use of popular generic forms which are playfully appropriated for their own fictional purposes, Noon's fictions *Vurt, Pollen* and *Nymphomation* combine classical myth and English folktale with drug fantasy, rave culture, cyberspace and overlays of *Alice's Adventures in Wonderland*; these genres fuse and blur, melting borders.

Science fiction is the most common genre used by cyberpunk writers; this is because it is a quintessentially modern genre, offering the chance to engage with contemporary scientific and technological ideas. The use of coded, *techno*, self-reflexive language which undoubtedly springs from postmodern concerns and writers' anxieties is explicit in cyberpunk fiction. And in a fiction of conspiracy theories and surveillance, it comes as no surprise that these writers use fictional techniques such as multiple points of view to illustrate multiple realities and multiple truths in their work which, in turn, is utilized in an eclectic fashion, amid kitsch and randomly overlapping forms of media.

Experiment with this: Learning to Experiment with Scientific and Technological Ideas in Fiction

Imagine a character in a novel who is in a computer game hacking through one system to another, discovering secret rooms and passageways, a web of interconnected worlds and 'other' characters. Write the scene using coded, techno, self-reflexive language to convey multiple points of view and multiple truths.

What Is True/What Is Not?

This chapter explores writing techniques and strategies that contemporary writers employ in order to experiment with truth claims within their postmodern fiction, so that writers and readers of experimental fiction can experiment with these techniques too.

What is true in a postmodern world?

Postmodernity depicts an era where there is a loss of faith not just in progress, but in authority and tradition, a shift in what people believe to be *true* and what people *actually* believe in. Once people lived within a single coherent worldview or truth; now people are living in a world of plurality, an 'over-exposure to otherness' (Trutti Anderson Postmodernism Reader, p. 6) and a 'barrage of cultural stimuli' (p. 9). And so, with access to a multiplicity of rituals and symbols, beliefs and values, new variations of old concepts, individuals are able to pick and mix worldviews and lifestyles, leading to concepts of truth being revised.

Whilst realism strives for an accepted truth, postmodern questions how to say something is true in a world which does not share an agreement on what truth is. And so, as people are rethinking and reshaping their worlds in random and eclectic ways, it begs the question is there anything that can be said to be *true* anymore?

Which *truths* are postmodern writers exploring in their fiction?

The point has already been made that postmodernity is an era when the keystones of the Enlightenment, the Grand Narratives, are no longer tenable; this is because they are not considered to be absolute truths.

This questioning of truth has impacted upon postmodern writers, and they are responding to these debates within their fiction, in particular the *truths* of science, history and religion.

What writing techniques are being used to investigate scientific theories?

For the postmodern writer, fragmentation is a celebration of the liberation from fixed beliefs and truths; because the *old truths* are being broken down, they are free to experiment by rewriting them, thereby creating new forms and new modes of expression. Postmodern writers playfully mix narratives, genres and discourses. This celebration of flexibility, play and self-reflexivity is a central element of postmodern fiction. Postmodern writers delight in playing with language, incorporating puns and language games within their work. In addition, by using 'intertextuality', a term coined in 1966 by Julia Kristeva to describe texts born out of, and referencing, other texts, so that a single limited viewpoint is not imposed in the traditional realist sense, the reader draws upon their own areas of knowledge, and in so doing, makes the text one's own.

Jeanette Winterson explores the difficulties in representing the truth, and questions what the truth actually is. Indeed, she highlights the possibility that there is not one universal truth; there is only the subjective truth and individual perception. As she writes in *Sexing the Cherry*, 'Did my childhood happen? I must believe it did, but I don't have any proof... Everyone remembers things which never happened...' (p. 92). Through her allusion to conflicting theories of time and space in this novel, Winterson claims that our subjective view is all we really have, hence the only version that we can relate to. 'In a night 2000,000 years can pass, time moving only in our minds' (p. 132).

In *Sexing the Cherry*, Winterson plays, interrogates and deconstructs scientific discourse. During the course of the narrative, she investigates the idea that time is an illusion and introduces the reader to the idea of alternative times: 'Every journey conceals another journey within its lines: the path not taken and the forgotten angle. These are the journeys I wish to record. Not the ones I made, but the ones I might have made, or perhaps did make in some other place or time' (Winterson, 1989, p. 9). Here, and throughout the text, she explores Einstein's theory of relativity, playing with the notion that past, present and future all co-exist, that time is an illusion and all there really is, is a continuous present: 'Thinking about time is like turning the globe round and round, recognizing that all journeys exist simultaneously, that to be in one place is not to deny the existence of another, even though that place cannot be felt or see' (Winterson, 1989, p. 89).

Coexisting times are continually referred to and by refusing to accept the traditional idea of past, present and future, she questions truth, 'Either we are all fantasists and liars or the past has nothing definite in it' (p. 92). At the beginning of the novel, she refers to the Hopi, a Native American tribe, who have, she says, 'a language as sophisticated as ours, but not tenses for past, present and future. The division does not exist. What does this say about time?' (Winterson, 1989, p. 7). Perhaps following Saussure, Winterson is making the claim that time and space can only be represented through language and since language is arbitrary to the extent that different languages have conflicting systems of representation, how can we ever begin to suggest that words have any direct link to the concept which they are trying to evoke?

In the Newtonian model of physics, there is only one reality at a time, absolute time and absolute space; everything in the universe is predictable and simple laws are all that are required to understand how it functions. However, quantum physics has challenged the Newtonian model, leading to a questioning of the certainties of time and space, resulting in the conclusion that multiple times and spaces do exist. As well as exploring Newton's scientific theories within *Sexing the Cherry*, Winterson also refers to the contradictory theory of quantum physics. So, what is quantum?

Quantum physics replaced the classical emphasis in science, on separate parts. Quantum is 'an entangled universe its many parts are interwoven, their boundaries and their identities overlap, and through their doing so a new reality is created' (Zohar, 1994, p. 258). The most revolutionary idea of quantum physics is that light is both 'wave-like' and 'particle-like' at the same time. In 1927, George Thompson proved the dual nature of electrons, known as 'wave-particle duality'. Electric charge travels as waves, both departs and arrives as particles and neither the 'wave-like' nor the 'particle-like' properties are more 'real'. Quantum actually refers to a packet of energy, an atom. Electrons, in a previously stable atom, may become unstable for no apparent reason, and there is no way of knowing by which path it may travel. However, the path will be discontinuous, behaving as though it is 'smeared out all over space and time, and is everything at once' (Zohar, 1994, p. 26). The electrons put out 'feelers' to see which path will suit best; these 'feelers' are known as virtual transitions and are the possible journeys which are made before something actual takes place. The actual journey the electron makes is known as a real transition. The existence of virtual states shows us that we can experience more than one reality at a time. Winterson alludes to this: 'I don't know if other worlds exist in space or time. Perhaps this is the only one and the rest is rich imaginings. Either way it doesn't matter. We have to protect both possibilities. They are independent' (Winterson, 1989, p. 128). Throughout *Sexing the Cherry*, Winterson illustrates that she is fully aware that what constitutes the real is now no longer straightforward. In fact, she expresses her belief in the real as being something that is 'multiple and complex' (Imagination and Reality 1995, p. 136). The concept of reality will be explored in the next chapter.

Experiment with this: Learning to Experiment with Time and Space

Time is an illusion: past, present and future all co-exist. Use this as a writing burst, that is, write without stopping, without censoring yourself, for ten minutes, using the sentence as a stimulus. Now re-write what you have written by crafting the creative writing into a non-linear text.

Experiment with this: Learning to Experiment with a Quantum World

'Postmodern fiction is fiction in a quantum universe' (Woods, 1999, p. 51).

Imagine a character who has just woken in a quantum world, one where all things are possible. Write a novel extract in which your character explores this world.

What writing techniques are being used to deconstruct religious doctrine?

'They say the postmodern individual is a member of many communities and networks, a participant in many discourses, an audience to messages from everybody and everywhere – messages that present conflicting ideals and norms and images of the world ... In the world of religion – or, to be more accurate, in the many worlds of religion – people are overhauling doctrines right and left. How could it be otherwise? If you regard the various truths and practices of a religion as socially constructed, you are likely to feel free to reconstruct them according to the needs (as you perceive them) of the present time' (Trutti p. 9).

Many writers in the twentieth century have deconstructed, rewritten and played with religious doctrine within their works. In *Life of Pi*, the writer Yann Martel, who was born in Spain but currently lives in Montreal, explores belief:

"Religion will save us," I said ...

"Religion?" Mr. Kumar grinned broadly. "I don't believe in religion. Religion is darkness."

Martel continues:

He spoke again. "Some people say God died during the Partition in 1947. He may have died in 1971 during the war. Or he may have died yesterday here in Pondicherry in an orphanage. That's what some people say, Pi. When I was your age, I lived in bed racked with polio. I asked myself every day, 'Where is God? Where is God? Where is God? God never came. It wasn't God who saved me – it was medicine'. (pp. 27–8)

Besides playing with scientific theories relating to time and space, Winterson deconstructs the *constructed truth* of religion within her fiction too. She sees biblical stories as powerful originators of narrative and seeks to celebrate, rather than contest, them in her work. She references Christianity and the mystic, shamanism and Buddhism, revelling in the mixing of narratives from diverse cultures, rewriting and recycling them, placing them in fragmented forms in contemporary contexts, showing them to be stories which can be manipulated as opposed to being fixed and given religious truths. Indeed, to be a postmodern writer is to become an archaeologist of narratives, a writer who discovers myths of the past, fits the fragments together and makes something new out of them.

Winterson is reacting to the relative truth of narratives of origin in her fiction; she uses myths ironically whilst still acknowledging the power of particular myths:

And so it was that on a particular day, some time later, she followed a star until it came to settle above an orphanage, and in that place was a crib, a child. A child with too much hair. (Winterson, 1985, p. 10)

The myth of the origin of the universe is a repeated motif in her work.

This is the theory.

In the beginning was a perfect ten-dimensional universe that cleaved into two. While ours, of three spatial dimensions and the oddity of time, expanded to fit our grossness, hers, of six-dimensions wrapped itself away in solitude.

This sister universe, contemplative, concealed, waits in our future as it as refused our past. It may be the symbol behind all our symbols. It may be the mandalas of the East and the Grail of the West. The clouded beauty that human beings have stared into since we learned to become conscious of our own face'. (Winterson, 1997, p. 4)

Winterson also recycles the myth of hell:

> The marriage of Heaven and Hell? The old sceptics used to say that if Hell exists, where is it? What part of the Universe does it occupy... The question 'Where is it' could not be answered satisfactorily. Many tried. Traditionally, the afterlife lairs at the centre of the earth: Odysseus got in through a cave entrance in Persephone's Grove, while Virgil and Dante had only to look under the floorboards in Italy. In 1714, an Englishman, Tobias Swinden, published his Enquiry In The Place Of Hell and concluded that Hell is on the sun. In 1740, Whiston, Newton's successor as professor Of Mathematics at Cambridge, proved that Hell was somewhere in the regions of Saturn. (Winterson, 1997, p. 3)

As can be seen, Winterson refutes linear expectations, rewriting biblical narratives, with humour, parody and repetition, mixing science and religion, fact and fiction and in so doing, questions all the old defining certainties: male/female, alive/dead, heaven/hell. This blending of styles and discourses, this blurring of boundaries and the rewriting and recycling of narratives is a crucial writing strategy that postmodern writers employ within their work, one experimental writers and readers of this book can incorporate into their writing practice. Postmodern fiction, and indeed Winterson, rewrites many discourses and truths, for example, religion, history, time and space, science, and in so doing, she creates work that is both stylistically and culturally pluralistic.

However, rewriting 'old' narratives and subverting conventional linear expectations leads critics to question whether writers such as Jeanette Winterson and Angela Carter, who, it has already been noted, rewrite fairy tales and 'own' their own stories, or whether they are simply fragments of recycled 'old' narratives. As a response to this criticism, it may be argued that writers who experiment with this practice reclaim the 'old' narratives by writing them anew, therefore making them their own. In all her fiction, Winterson is concerned with cultural and philosophical debates and corresponds with Lyotard's notion of collapsing of Grand Narratives into meta-narratives. Her fiction refutes stability and fixity. The reader most certainly has to engage with, and interpret, her work, create one's own meaning, whilst enjoying the playfulness and plurality that this experience evokes.

Experiment with this: Learning to Rewrite Old Narratives of Religion

Rewrite the biblical story of Adam and Eve, put it in a contemporary setting, blend discourses, use humour, subvert linear expectations, and in so doing, create a new story.

Experiment with this: Learning to Use Language Games, Puns and Intertextuality

Rewrite the Noah's Ark biblical story and inscribe it with language games, puns and incorporate intertextuality in the retelling.

In *Sum*, the author David Eagleman rewrites stories of the afterlife: I won't die, I'll live forever as a download ... Use this as a starting point for a short story.

How is the concept of history portrayed in postmodern fiction?

Postmodern fiction is an art form which problematizes the making of both history and fiction. And within postmodern works, history can be seen as a narrative form rather than a collection of *proven* facts. 'One of the thrusts of postmodernist revisionist history is to call into question the reliability of official history. The postmodernists fictionalise history, but by doing so they imply that history itself may be a form of fiction'

(McHale, 1987, p. 96). And as William Gibson says, 'History itself is seen to be even more obviously a construct, subject to revision' (Distrust That Particular Flavour, p. 52). History, then, is no longer a concept that progresses through time; it is simply a set of stories or myths resounding in the present.

Postmodern fiction, therefore, can be viewed as an investigation into ways in which narrative constructs, and reflects upon, history; it recycles history for consumption, deconstructing both history and fiction, thereby remaking them. Many theorists, including Baudrillard, have argued that postmodern fiction appropriates history to create an anti-historical fiction. Fiction remakes the past as nostalgia, linking it with eclectic modes of consumer, information, mass media, popular culture and a service-orientated society. The very fact that postmodern fiction is self-referential and self-reflexive severs the text from actual historical reality, making the fiction into a formalist exercise, one which is not directly related to its social conditions of production. However, while postmodern fiction severs a simple relationship with history, it does attempt to explore different histories.

The genre of fabulist fiction or magic realism opposes traditional realist fiction by its critique of the myth of history as a set of *proven* facts; for example, in *Invisible Cities*, Italian writer Italo Calvino uses the imaginary conversations of the 'characters' of Marco Polo and Kublain Khan to underline the questionable concept of history. He does this by mixing historical detail, for example, thirteenth-century Marco Polo describes airports and skyscrapers he has seen in cities whilst travelling Khan's vast empire. Also, by using historical figures, Calvino, the writer, adopts a philosophical, historical stance, one which revises the modern conception of history. It appears that it is only possible to view the present in relation to the past; so there seems little point in representing history. The reader, and for that matter, the writer, is not merely experiencing history, merely using incidents to understand our present predicament. Where postmodernism recognizes a continuum and progression from the past, it subverts the practices of traditional modernist frameworks in order to subordinate history, seeing it simply as a fiction.

What narrative strategies are utilized in the revision of history?

Calvino employs a number of narrative strategies and techniques to manipulate the historical content of *Invisible Cities*, and in so doing, he creates his own version of history, a new history. He does this by fragmenting the cities in order to express the impossibility of discovering an absolute truth. He also juxtaposes the variety of narratives and the cities, employing author intrusion and intertexuality, as well as establishing mood, rather than plot, which establishes the postmodern nature of *Invisible Cities*; in addition, this serves to create metanarratives and dislocation. By his revision of Marco Polo and Khan, Calvino is subverting the traditional view of history, that is, a history which is traditionally viewed as linear. However, with the juxtaposition of narratives, Calvino creates a non-linear text, implying, perhaps influenced by Lyotard's claim, that history has ceased to exist; therefore, for the reader, it is impossible to fix meaning; the text is writerly because of the plurality of realities contained within each city. For example, within *Invisible Cities*, there is the city of Zirma, in which there is 'a blind black man shouting in the crowd, a lunatic teetering on a skyscraper's cornice, a girl walking with a puma on a leash … streets of shops where tattoos are drawn on sailors' skin; underground trains crammed with obese women suffering from humidity' (p. 19). As David Lyon says, 'the world of meaning fractures and fragments, making it hard even to speak of meanings traditionally conceived' (Postmodernity, p. 11).

Experiment with this: Learning to Re-tell History and Experiment with Juxtapositions of Narratives to Create a Non-linear Text

Adopt two historical characters from two different periods of history. What are their stories? Write them, real or imagined. Revise the stories, juxtaposing the stories each tells the other about their lives, to create a non-linear text.

Experiment with this: Learning to Create a Writerly Text

Invent a city. Give it a name. Create a piece of fiction about this city, one like Calvino's Zirma, in which there exists a plurality of realities.

What Is Real/What Is Not?

This chapter investigates a postmodern worldview where perceptions of reality are constantly shifting; it reflects upon how the ever-intrusive media has led to a world of simulacra, a society saturated in simulations, a world where the *real* disappears behind the image. It also explores postmodern writers who question the nature of reality by showing that it is simply a construct within their fiction, and it investigates their writing techniques and strategies that enable them to do this.

What is *the real* in the postmodern era?

In the postmodern era, we are living with a multiplicity of realities and selves, raising questions about the nature of reality, language and human nature. As David Lyon's writes, 'One of the most basic themes of postmodern debate revolves around reality or multiplicity of realities' (David Lyon, 1994, p. 7).

In the twentieth century, the question is asked: How *real* can reality be when history is actually a story because it relies upon language? As Saussure suggests, language is arbitrary. In the twentieth century, the way reality is constituted questions all the key elements of the Enlightenment, that is, the Grand Narratives of religion, scientific progress, history. So, if all the Enlightenment realities are obsolete, what is left: Baudrillard's hyperreality?

The development of the media opens up an increased exposure to a multiplicity of perspectives undermining any belief in one true reality. In the world of media, reality and fantasy break down and are replaced by hyperreality, a world of self-referential signs, that is, signs referring to other signs – a world of simulacra, where the distinction between objects and their representations is dissolved, signs lose contact with things signified. TV advertisements are prime examples; flickering images, endeavouring to sell commodities, erode the distinction between the real world and that of the media, leaving us with Baudrillard's hyperreality. 'The sign has become reality, or the hyperreal; the sign, that is, masks the fact that there is no basic reality' (Jean Baudrillard, Simulations. Semiotext, p. 1).

Society is saturated with simulations so that the *real* dissolves behind the image. Each day we live through a collage of visual images: TV, cinema, advertisements. This brings into question the notion of reality, and this may be one way of seeing the postmodern, as a debate about reality. The idea that reality is broken down into many images is common within postmodern discourse, which begs the question: What is more real, the *actual* or the simulation? Baudrillard argues that Disneyland and theme parks are a 'substitute for a diminishing sense of reality (p. 1), whilst Umberto Eco, the Italian novelist, believes that 'technology can give more reality than nature can' (Eco, Travels In Hyppereality, p. 44). Debates are explored through fiction by some writers; for example, in his novel *White Noise* (1985) in Chapter 7, Don DeLillo illustrates that the publication of erotic letters in magazines may be more stimulating for their authors than the actual erotic experiences themselves; the idea being that the simulation replaces reality. This leads the reader to actively engage in the text by provoking them to ask the question: What is more real, the *actual* experiences or the publication of those experiences?

How do postmodern writers illustrate the impact of the media?

In *White Noise*, DeLillo investigates a society suffused with simulacra. Indeed, this novel is a creative study of the impact the media has on society, a society permeated with signs and images. Specifically, DeLillo explores the difficulty of choosing relevant, meaningful messages from the 'White Noise'. Through the use of dialogue, DeLillo explores the idea that *real* events are constructed and interpreted through the media; therefore, they are only simulations of *real* events. For example, in Chapter 6, the character Jack drives his son, Heinrich, to school. Heinrich informs Jack that the radio said it was going to rain. Jack says that it is already raining, and that they don't need to believe the radio over their own senses. However, Heinrich believes senses can lie and he refutes Jack's argument. So, here the reader observes father and son debating the objectivity of reality, and posing the question: What is real and what is not? Is it what the characters experience through their senses? Or is it what they are told by the media? The reader is being shown two different versions of reality. Jack believes the reality of the senses to be more real, whereas Heinrich believes the reality of the media is more real. What does the reader believe?

Experiment with this: Learning to Investigate Simulation Through Dialogue

Select a tourist site anywhere in the world. Imagine a character in a novel who is visiting this site. This character has only visited the gift shop, but they consider that they have experienced the *real* tourist site. Write a postcard from the character to their friend back home. Now imagine this: The friend, who has actually been to the site, receives the postcard; a telephone conversation between the two friends ensues, one in which they discuss their experiences of the tourist site. Write the conversation.

Experiment with this: Learning to Explore the *Real* Through Dialogue

Choose a *real* event that has been in the media in 2012. Imagine you are a journalist in a novel who is on a chat show on television. Through dialogue, re-tell this event to the viewers in the studio and those watching television. By using dialogue, write the conversations which display the reactions of the viewers in the studio, those watching at home and the characters who were involved in the *real* event.

Experiment with this: Learning to Examine the Media Through Dialogue

Imagine two characters who are watching the weather forecast on TV. They are told it has been hot sun for days and this will continue for today, but it has been, and still is, raining. The friends had planned a picnic, one wants to go on the picnic, but the other does not, because of the rain. Write the conversation.

How do signs, images and slogans become the *real* in a postmodern world?

The saturation of images, texts and narratives, together with consumer and entertainment choices, has created a 'living symbiosis between industry, consumer and culture…the market itself becomes the greatest reality for a growing number in society' (W Raeper, A Brief Guide To Ideas (Oxford, 1991, p. 334)). This is another theme explored in *White Noise*, the idea that the marketplace has become the *real* reality for many consumers.

Shopping has become an experience of spectacle, where the customer can gaze at a glittering array of goods and images under the gaze of high-tech electronic surveillance within a climate-controlled, theme-park-inspired environment and this is the case for Wilder, a character in *White Noise*. Shopping, acquiring certain consumer items, is the greatest reality for Wilder. When he takes items off supermarket shelves, he becomes a symbol for the unthinking consumer. Having a limited vocabulary, Wilder thinks his consumer items speak for him, through their signs, images and slogans; they tell *real* stories about him. So, by acquiring the items, Wilder epitomizes the item's reality; the item is him; and he is it. However, Jack wants to believe that human beings actually have an innate sense of reality, a common sense, intuitive version, and yet, Nazism disproves this notion. In the novel, DeLillo shows how Nazism illustrates how society is easily controlled by images and spectacle. So again the reader is left pondering: How is reality constructed?

Experiment with this: Learning to Use Signs and Images in Fiction

Imagine a scene from a novel set in a city where the abundant signs and images impact upon a character's attitudes and behaviour. How and why do they impact upon the character? Write the scene.

How is reality constructed within postmodern fiction?

Postmodern writers continually search and experiment with fresh forms, and new techniques, within their fiction, to enable readers to see how reality is constructed within their works; it also seeks to remind readers that they are simply reading fiction, which is, in itself, a construct. For example, at the opening of *If on a Winter's Night a Traveller*, Calvino tells his readers: 'You are about to begin reading Italo Calvino's new novel, *If on a winter's night a traveller*' (p. 1).

In their fiction, postmodern writers employ a technique called *ostranenie*, that is, the deformation of ordinary language – a technique identified by Viktor Shklovsky from the Russian Formalist school of thought. This technique seeks to make the habitual unfamiliar, thereby making reader see things differently and anew, so perceptions are kept fresh. Jon McGregor uses this technique at the beginning of *If Nobody Speaks of Remarkable Things*:

> If you listen, you can hear it.
> The city, it sings. (p. 1).

The writing devices, then, de-familiarize the reader's automized conventions or perceptions and 'make forms difficult, to increase the difficulty and length of perception because the process of perception is an aesthetic end in itself and must be prolonged'. 'Art is a way of experiencing the artfulness of an object; the object is not important...' (Viktor Shklovsky, *Art as Technique* (1917)). Shklovsky's theory shows the reader that all versions of reality are constructed, that a literary text is not unified and organic; rather it is composed of various kinds of writing, techniques and devices, which can be assembled and interpreted in various ways. By drawing attention to its devices, an anti-realist or an experimental work of fiction is produced, which conveys plot as being just a vehicle for the devices. And as David Lodge says: 'An experimental novel is one that ostentatiously deviates from the received ways of representing reality – either in narrative organisation or in style, or in both – to heighten or change our perception of that reality' (David Lodge, The Art of Fiction, p. 105).

How does a postmodern writer de-familiarize, and play with, a reader's perceptions of reality?

In *Slaughterhouse-Five*, the breakdown of a single reality drives the novel, with Kurt Vonnegut compelling the reader to question not only the novel's realism, but reality itself; it leads the reader into a state of uncertainty, one of unfamiliarity, so much so that they are unsure where the real experience ends and the imagination begins. Vonnegut's activity of relaying personal experience to the reader allows him to experiment with a move away from traditional fiction to a form where the author and reader, to a certain extent, become characters within the novel. Vonnegut is capturing an unreal experience, and he engages the reader to experience this unfamiliar reality by using a number of narrative strategies. The protagonist Billy is out of time; he experiences past and future events out of sequence and repetitively following a non-linear narrative. Vonnegut lays bare his technique in the novel, reminding the reader that they are reading a fiction by inviting them to observe the process and not to *get lost* in the narrative.

Experiment with this: Learning to De-familiarize a Reader's Perceptions of Reality

'All this happened, more or less'. But it was in 1962. The going to work part that morning was true. A guy really was killed in the street by a hired gunman. Another guy I knew really did go AWOL 'I've changed all the names'. I thought it would be easy for me to re-tell the tale in a fiction. After all, I am a writer. 'Listen: Billy Pilgrim has come unstuck in time'. He has gone to sleep an old man and awakened on that day…

Using this as a starting point, tell the story…

Giving a Voice to *Other*

This chapter explores how some historical changes have led to a multicultural society, and how, in turn, this has impacted on postmodern fiction; in addition, it investigates the techniques postmodern writers employ, so experimental readers and writers of fiction can incorporate them into their writing practice too.

In the twentieth century, there have been profound historical changes which have impacted on the world of fiction. These significant changes, in particular the end of the Empire and the rise of the Black Power movement in the United States, have led to a significant increase in awareness in terms of racial identity. Throughout the last century, more and more people, for a variety of reasons – for example, political, and the acceleration of technology – have been crossing national and cultural borders. Indeed, borders are no longer so easily definable.

Globalization has led to a rise in multiculturalism and cultural hybridity, terms associated with celebrating our postmodern, postcolonial world, a world which is now a rich melting pot of cultures, a world concerned with multiple, *other* voices, finding their own individual voice. As American artist Alex Grey writes, '… postmodern pluralism embraces so many maverick points of view it can generate tolerance toward cultural difference' (Alex Grey, The Mission of Art, p. 15).

This postmodern era of transition brings once marginalized voices into the mainstream and celebrates their difference. As a result, writing coming out of this postmodern era has a strong sense of being in the process of change and portrays a world far less coherent and easily definable than previously. The construction of an *other* voice is a central element of postmodern fiction; this *other* voice is a voice which permits expression, negotiation, transformation and change. However, how was this *other* voice experienced in realist fiction?

How are *other* voices experienced in realist fiction?

Displacement is something many people encounter as a result of being uprooted from their place of birth. Some people voluntarily migrate or they are forcibly uprooted in search of work, a new way of life or escape from their countries because of war. As a consequence, themes of racism and exile, displacement and migration are common in the Commonwealth Literature of the 1980s. The Jamaican novelist Joan Riley's *The Unbelonging* (1985), for example, deals primarily with the experience of an eleven-year-old girl, Hyacinth, who moved from exuberant Kingston to the less colourful Britain and the problems and adjustments she faced. A dominant theme of the writer Caryl Philips' work is also one of displacement. This is the result of having been born in St Kitts in the eastern Caribbean to parents with roots in India, Africa and Madeira and growing up in Britain. This leads him to research the history of the slave trade in order to understand his identity; this becomes a backdrop for a number of his novels. V. S. Naipaul's *The Enigma of Arrival* (1987) and Timothy Mo's *Sweet Sour* (1982) all explore notions of displacement in realist forms. However, some writers have observed and experienced a shift in displacement and this has implications for their writing practice.

What is the shift in displacement?

As a result of the breakdown in the old truth claims and all the old certainties, identity is no longer fixed in terms of cultural roles; as a result, there is a shift in the way unbelonging is viewed so that individuals are free to explore and rejoice in difference. Postmodernism takes the idea of a fragmented self with the sense of displacement, veering in a positive direction, rather than one which is angst ridden. Here, the idea of displacement, seen as being negative in the traditional sense, is seen to be liberating and the idea of belonging to be simply a myth of origins. In the postmodern world, perspectives of the migrant, opposed to giving cause for lamentation, can be viewed as giving cause for celebration.

How are postmodern writers exploring displacement?

In true postmodern fashion, in his novel *Midnight's Children*, 1981, the Anglo-Indian writer Salman Rushdie celebrates displacement, fragmented self and cultural difference, besides exploring colonialism, independence and the partition of India. *Midnight's Children* is a novel of international modern history, a vast postmodern construct of oral and written narratives from the multi-cultural tradition. The narrative is told by Saleem Sinai and is set in the actual historical events. Saleem is born at midnight, 15 August 1947, when India gains independence from British colonial rule. Saleem has telepathic powers; he can hear the voices of the other 'midnight's children', all born in that initial hour and all endowed with magical gifts. The book teems with these *other* voices, celebrating, in fictional terms, myriad life and language in conflict with an oppressive centre; in so doing, he creates a text which celebrates the inclusion of the marginalized, seeing them as valid opinions on the world. Saleem uses his telepathic powers to assemble a Midnight's Children's Conference. The aim of this conference is to reflect on the issues the diverse nation, India, faces in its early statehood, issues concerning linguistic, religious, cultural and political differences.

In 1988, Rushdie published *Satanic Verses* to great controversy in the Muslim community. This book deals with the immigrant experience in Britain. *Satanic Verses* explores how migration fosters an awareness that perceptions of reality are fragile and that the politics of religion are manipulative; it also criticises Western materialism. One of the most important premises of the book is that migrants are defined by their *otherness* as a people where fusions occur, that is, unions between what they were and where they find themselves. This hybridity is inevitable and to be celebrated. On television, the character Saladin Chamcha sees a tree growing in England, which he thinks can take the place of a tree his father chopped down in India:

> If such a tree were possible, then so was he; he, too, could cohere, send down roots, survive. Amid all the televisual images of hybrid tragedies – the uselessness of mermen, the failures of plastic surgery, the Esperanto-like vacuity of much modern art, the Coca-Colonization of the planet – he was given this one gift. (p. 94)

Experiment with this: Learning to Experiment with Hybridity

Write an interior monologue in which a character reflects and celebrates their hybridity, by reflecting on their cultural history, that is, their past, and where they find themselves now, in the present.

Hanif Kureishi, an Anglo-Pakistani writer, confronts racial identity and the experience of the immigrant in *The Buddha of Suburbia* (1990). Karim Amir, the protagonist, 'an Englishman born and bred, almost', is a hybrid of Asian and British, one who is searching for a sense of belonging. 'The odd mixture of continents and blood, of here and there, of belonging and not' (p. 3). The book illustrates that there is no fixed self, only innumerable ways of being. Cultural identity is portrayed as being unstable and in a state of transformation, something complex involving new ways of being, resulting in new identities. And the two identities, English and Pakistan, will merge and come together in a new identity.

More recently, *White Teeth* (2000) by Zadie Smith has been hailed as the first black British novel. This narrative explores how history is used and misused, how it affects young people growing up and how they deal with the desire to know their history and to be freed from it. There are stories of three families across numerous generations, linking them to the Caribbean, Bangladesh and India, and via the Second World War, to Italy and Bulgaria. The novel is not so much postmodern in its techniques and strategies, but it deals with the content of a postmodern world, one that is shaped by a cultural mix: Chalfens, a well-established family; Marcus Chalfen's son described as a 'cross pollination between a lapsed-Catholic horticulturalist feminist and an intellectual Jew' (Smith 2000, p. 267). His family's immigration to Britain took place earlier than the Jamaican Jones' and the Bangladeshi Iqbal's. All three families make up a London of social and cultural mix and ongoing change. They're creating a space in which different races and colours of skin are strangers alike, where contrasting first and last names reflect a mix of history, culture and religion. *White Teeth* celebrates a metropolis where all strangers are at home, where different heritages can exist side by side in the same neighbourhood, within the same household and even within the same person. Cultural hybridity can exist even if tensions are apparent, but it suggests that change is possible and new spaces of transformation are possible; society can be changed, shaped and re-formed by cultural diversity.

What techniques and strategies are postmodern writers experimenting within postcolonial fiction?

In his fiction, Rushdie illustrates that diverse cultures present different ways of viewing the world and that cultural diversity is to be celebrated. 'The world was new again' (*Midnight's Children*, p. 12). The postcolonial style portrayed in Rushdie's fiction utilizes eclecticism: Hindu myth is juxtaposed with Bombay cinema and cartoon strips, whilst Islamic lore is juxtaposed against third-world magic realism.

The effect of magic realism calls into question the boundary between fiction and truth. Based on the early life of Rushdie, *Midnight's Children* is a blend of fiction, politics and magic, making the reader aware of the changes in India in the twentieth century. Rushdie undermines the concept of historical truth as recorded fact and presents a multiplicity of histories. He weaves a text that fuses tradition and current cultural influences to create an open-ended, postcolonial discourse. Likewise in *Satanic Verses*, inspired by the life of Muhammad, Rushdie, once again, blends fact and fiction; for example, Farishta is a Bollywood superstar and is based on Indian film stars. Magic realism is interweaved with subplots that are narrated as dream visions. There are intertextual references, including mythology and popular culture (esp. Chapter VII). He also employs a comic tone and uses irony and satire. In addition, he uses the concept of defamiliarization, by playing with the readers' perceptions, subverting expectations: 'I was born in the city of Bombay... once upon a time' (p. 9).

Experiment with this: Learning to Experiment with Intertextuality to Create a Postcolonial Fiction

Using 'I was born in the city of...' as a starting point for a piece of fiction, utilize Hindu myth juxtaposed with fact, Bollywood cinema, magic realism and history to create an intertextual postcolonial text.

In sharp contrast to Rushdie's fiction, Kureishi's *The Buddha of Suburbia* is written in a realist style and has a strong autobiographical content. However, it is an example of a postcolonial novel because of its content; the book parodies the postcolonial and ironizes ethnicity. It is a novel which explores Karim growing up and the transformation of his environment. Kureishi uses juxtaposition, collage and many cultural signifiers, especially those associated with popular music, to investigate a young man being both 'here and there' both 'belonging and not'.

Experiment with this: Learning to
Experiment with Eclecticism to
Create a Postcolonial Text

Employ juxtaposition, collage and cultural signifiers to explore the
world of a young person growing up in Britain in the late eighties, a
young person who is both 'here and there' both 'belonging and not'.

Further Reading

Anderson, Truett (1996) Postmodernism Reader, London: Fontana Press.

Auster, Paul (1987) The New York Trilogy, London: Faber & Faber.

Calvino, Italo (1972) Invisible Cities, London: Secker and Warburg.

—— (1982) If on a Winter's Night a Traveller, London: Picador.

Carter, Angela (1979) The Bloody Chamber, London: Penguin Books.

Coupland, Douglas (1992) Generation X, London: Abacus.

DeLillo, Don (1985) White Noise, London: Picador.

Ellis Easton, Bret (1991) American Psycho, London: Picador.

Gibson, William (1984) Neuromancer, London: Viking.

—— (2012) Distrust That Particular Flavour, London: Viking.

Gregson, Ian (2004) Postmodern Literature, London: Hodder Headline.

Kureishi, Hanif (1990) The Buddha of Suburbia, London: Faber & Faber.

Lodge, David (1992) The Art of Fiction, London: Penguin Books.

Lyon, David (1994) Postmodernity, Buckingham: Open University Press.

Martel, Yann (2002) Life of Pi, Edinburgh: Canongate.

McGregor, Jon (2003) If Nobody Speaks of Remarkable Things, London:
    Bloomsbury.

—— (2012) This Isn't the Sort of Thing That Happens to Someone Like You,
    London: Bloomsbury.

Noon, Jeff (1996) Automated Alice, London: Transworld.

Palahniuk, Chuck (1997) Fight Club, London: Vintage.

Potter, Dennis (1973) Hide and Seek, London: Faber & Faber.

Riley, Joan (1985) The Unbelonging, London: The Women's Press.

Rushdi, Salman (1995) Midnight's Children, London: Vintage.

Sutherland, Luke (2004) Venus As a Boy, London: Bloomsbury.

Vonnegut, Kurt (1991) Slaughterhouse-Five, London: Vintage.

Winter, Kathleen (2011) Annabel, London: Jonathan Cape.

Winterson, Jeanette (1985) Oranges Are Not the Only Fruit, London: Pandora Press.

—— (1989) Sexing the Cherry, London: Vintage.

—— (1996) Art Objects, London: Vintage.

Woods, Tim (1999) Beginning Postmodernism, Manchester: Manchester University Press.

Section Four

A New Era Is Dawning

This section will explore the shifting technological, cultural and spiritual climate of the twenty-first century which is pushing fiction into a *new*, exciting realm, so that experimental readers of fiction can understand what these works are doing, and how. There will also be creative writing exercises to enable writers to experiment with the writing techniques and strategies that are explored within the following chapters.

What is the New Era?

Postmodernism called for a re-evaluation of power; it sought to de-privilege any one meaning so that all discourses were equally valid which led to marginalized groups being given their voice. However, increasingly artistic success has become about money; art has become a business, leading to a conflict of interest, and as a result, some writers have come to judge, and measure, their own success and worth by financial gain. This provokes the question: are we left with nothing but the market? And is this the opposite of what postmodernism originally intended? Postmodernism's influence has been everywhere and has been the dominant concept of late twentieth and early twenty-first centuries, and yet, there now appears to be a need to respond and react to something other, but what?

Certainties have changed. With the complete breakdown of Grand Narratives, our beliefs about time and space, science and religion, reality and illusion, life and death, and the nature of consciousness have changed in ways that we have never experienced before.

The twenty-first century is a time of political unrest, war in Iraq and Afghanistan, recession, credit crunch, unemployment, repossessions, reality TV, celebrity culture, coalition government, euro zone debt crisis and rapid technological growth. There is a lack of borders, an amalgamation of cultures and migration, so that many people do not know their extended or immediate family history.

These are times when we *really* are not sure what is real or true anymore, a time when the boundaries of art, reality and celebrity, advertising, marketing and publicity are becoming increasingly blurred. The current generation has grown up with digital culture. There is virtual and augmented reality – Facebook, Myspace, Bebo, Twitter, Skype. People are able to portray multiple, edited representations of themselves on screen. What then are the implications for a life lived out through a computer interface: instant access to friendships all around the world, constant connectedness, online predators, ubiquitous information, instant gratification, knowledge, cyber bullying, paranoia, or all of these?

New technology allows us to send multiple messages, simultaneous texts, emails and tweets; this has implications for the present moment, leading the present and also reality to be the virtual. Exposure to technology is shifting the hard wiring of the brain; our thoughts are speeding up to cope with the vast amount of information we access, and process, in any one day. We are living in a 24/7 fast-paced, fast-food, fast-changing transient, pinging, beeping, lack of space, lack of silence, lack of solitude world, where, as the film director David Fincher suggests, private behaviour has now become a relic of another era.

This is a time when it appears that capitalism promotes individualism over the collective needs of society, a society that appears to value money, youth, fame and beauty above all else. It seems the twenty-first century is a time of confusion about consumer culture and values. On the one hand, the self-obsessive slogan *Because I'm worth it*! views consumption as a right, not a luxury, and the desire for instant gratification as being of the utmost importance. And yet, on the other hand, there is a curious restlessness within society, a sense that we need to change our values.

We are living in a post-Christian world where there appears to be a yearning for what some deem authenticity and for what others deem meaning. The landscape literature writer Robert Macfarlane, author of *The Old Ways: A Journey on Foot*, suggests that even though church-going figures have fallen, people are ever increasingly seeking to go on pilgrimage. Indeed, the British writer Rachel Joyce's *The Unlikely Pilgrimage of Harold Fry* long listed for the Booker Prize in 2011 is testimony to Macfarlane's suggestion. The protagonist of this book, Harold Fry, leaves home one morning to post a letter and keeps walking from one end of Britain to the other; in his eyes, he is walking to save his friend's life. He is on a pilgrimage.

In the twenty-first century, there is a strong desire for individuals to escape the urban and glimpse an untamed world, to reconnect with lost instincts; in turn this is linked with concerns for the environment and displacement. Environmental, cultural and economic factors are combining to make people re-think their lives. There are numerous campaigns for supporting environmental issues, for example, ecotricity, that is, making electricity powered by windmills. Also, there is an increase in the use of solar power and an intention to harness wave power. Growing organic food on shared allotments or keeping chickens and ducks for their free-range eggs have become popular pursuits.

More nature reserves are evolving and more people are enjoying outdoor pursuits. Cycling has been embraced with enthusiasm, with the government promoting benefits for those who cycle to work; it has been said, *Driving Is the New Smoking*. Government campaigns, such as 5 A Day fruits and vegetables, incite healthy eating. There are smoking bans in public places and frequent advice is to be found encouraging us to give up smoking and to carefully monitor our alcohol consumption.

Walking and running have also become very popular, not only for health reasons but also for their spiritual value; as Macfarlane has noted these pursuits offer freedom from the pressures of day-to-day life. There are even those who deem the act of walking an art form, for example, Richard Long, whose work maps territories from Dartmoor to the Andes. On his journeys, Long has arranged stones by roads, aligned pebbles in river beds, traced furrows in sand; he records this work in photographs and descriptions and it was exhibited at the Hepworth, Wakefield: June to October, 2012.

Fashion designers are using eco-friendly materials. The concept *Fact Fashion* has been developed. *Fact Fashion* not only focuses on materials, and the way clothes are made, but it also addresses issues such as homelessness, drugs, poverty; facts such as *Every two minutes someone loses their home* are being inscribed on garments. Building upon Anita Roddick's *The Body Shop* concept, there are more and more eco products on the market. Established in 1992 by the European Commission, a logo now appears on 17,000 products and services across Europe, EU Ecolabel, which identifies products and services as having a reduced impact on the environment. It is even possible to stay on an EU Ecolabel-approved campsite. In addition, there are increasing numbers of recycling bins and less packaging on products, and blogs to combat climate change encourage cycling to work and consumers to buy fair-trade products. Celebrities are becoming more and more involved in charity events, taking their lead from Bob Geldof's *Live Aid*. There are fundraising events like *Children In Need* and *Red Nose Day*, and sponsored runs, walks and swims.

Currently, television programmes such as Mary Beard's *Meet the Romans* are hugely popular, as is the series *Who Do You Think You Are?* The popularity of such television series illustrates society's interest in identity and history. Other programmes which reflect other contemporary cultural concerns and interests include *Britain's Lost Routes*, in which Griff Rhys Jones embarks on a trek from Holywell to St David's in the style of a medieval pilgrimage. And there are programmes like the fashionable Professor Brian Cox's *The Wonders of the Universe*, David Attenborough's *Life on Earth* and Simon Reeve's *Indian Ocean* – programmes which urge the viewer and reader (there are book spin-offs too) to enjoy the planet, whilst at the same time advocate that we treat it responsibly. There are dramas such as the supernatural French series *The Returned*, which deals with issues such as grief, loss and the spiritual concept of resurrection. There are celebrities such as

Richard Gere and David Lynch who promote the Buddhist concept of mindfulness as a way of life. And there is an increasing interest in holistic therapies: yoga and acupuncture, Indian head massage and hot stone treatments, reflexology and reiki. In addition, there is a school of thought which advocates that we need to equip ourselves with emotional intelligence, which, in turn, should be integrated into our political and economic thinking to create a society which includes more compassion and inclusion.

What implications does the New Era have for the content of fiction?

The New Era, which has been outlined, has a number of implications for the writer; for example, it is clearly affecting the content of fiction being created. Currently, there is a wave of fiction which appears to be reacting to the shallowness of postmodern fiction; this new wave asks big questions such as, What is the meaning of life? It is fiction that it is searching for meaning and something to believe in whilst also acknowledging the spiritual, for example, the work of David Mitchell, Grace McCleen, Samantha Harvey, Scarlett Thomas and David Eagleman, the fiction that will be investigated in the chapter: Beyond Postmodernism. The contemporary literature resonates with some modern fiction, dominant themes of Virginia Woolf's fiction; for example, *Mrs Dalloway, To the Lighthouse, Voyage Out* and *Jacob's Room* also revolve around a search for the meaning of life.

The classics are also making a comeback; writers such as Hilary Mantel, twice Booker Prize winner, and Mary Renault are reflecting our renewed interest in history. Likewise, Madeline Miller's debut novel, *The Song of Achilles,* won the Orange prize for fiction in June 2012. The *Iliad* also inspired David Malouf's 2009 novel *Random* and poet Alice Oswald's *Memorial,* 2011, which are also re-workings of the original poem. This engagement with the classics also links with philosophical questions and connections that many of the noted classics are exploring, for example: What it is to be human? Also, in terms of the *Iliad*, the theme of war has particular relevance for a twenty-first-century readership where readers have become accustomed to seeing news coverage of conflicts in Afghanistan and Iraq; Miller has said that she was aware of the parallels when writing *The Song of Achilles*.

What implications does the New Era have for the form of fiction?

In addition to this shift in content, there is also a shift in the form of fiction. How has this come about? Fundamentally, the advances in technology and social media have impacted hugely on the ways fiction is now being created; for example, YouTube blurs the distinction between artist and consumer, leading to extra *new* creative forms and outpourings. People all over the world, via the internet, can collaborate on art works, so that there are a multiplicity of authors for a text; for example, the *Johnny Cash Project* and the *Life and Day Project*, a film portrait that gives fragmented views of our world and lives, and blurs the boundary between artist and consumer. Likewise, the documentary *Britain in a Day*, directed by Ridley Scott and Morgan Matthews, is a very similar project. On Saturday 12 November 2011, at the invitation of the directors, an eclectic range of British people captured their lives, the mundane, exciting, strange and amazing on camera. The text, crafted from more than 750 hours of footage including 11,526 clips submitted to YouTube, offers a view of twenty-first-century life in the UK. After the Olympics, an online archive was launched to showcase the full-length submissions from which this film is created. Some fiction also experiments with this inclusive creative process; narratives are created online using a plurality of authors. And so, it can be seen that ways of producing and distributing works are changing, all of which have impacted upon the form of fiction. There is a form known as Collaborative Fiction Writing. Ken Kesey experimented with this form in 1989 to produce a text, *Caverns*, one that had been created by himself and a creative writing class he taught. Since 2007, there has been Protagonize, a Collaborative Fiction Writing Community online, in which one author begins a story and others post different branches or chapters to it.

It is also interesting to note that the content of fiction can often be inspired by new technologies, for example, Pulitzer Prize winner Jennifer Egan's Twitter fiction: *Black Box*.

There are now many alternative ways of making fiction and art works which have impacted on the way the reader/viewer absorbs creativity; these are often collaborative and interdisciplinary in nature. For example, the *First Cut* exhibition, at Manchester City Art gallery (October 2012 to January 2013), features work by contemporary artists who have been significantly inspired by the acts of writing and reading. Su Blackwell gives form to the scenes we imagine when we read literature. She cuts out imagery from books to create three-dimensional tableaux which are then placed inside display boxes. Fairy tales and folklore are rich subjects for Blackwell, although she does not exclusively use children's books. In the work *Wuthering Heights*, 2010, she presents her interpretation of the moorland farmhouse of the title. Georgina Russell dissects and reconstructs old, discarded books from the cannon of literature. Whereas Chris Kenny, inspired by the Dadaists' love of chance and randomness, collects phrases and sentences from hundreds of secondhand books, he then re-presents and subverts these text fragments, and constructs surreal narratives. In Rob Ryan's works, text and imagery are entwined to highlight the importance of language. French artist Beatrice Coron's work is inspired by everything she reads and contains various narratives: playful, but also macabre and challenging. Long-Bin Chen from Taiwan is inspired by the texts rendered obsolete in the face of our increasingly digital word; he recycles books to give them meaning. Andrea Dezso from Romania creates non-linear narratives which have a surreal quality. She is not prescriptive about how the works should be read, but invites the reader to create their own stories around the characters and environments, based upon their own dreams and experiences. And

Danish siblings Martin and Line Anderson bring to life a novel by one of New Zealand's most revered authors, Maurice Gee. The work entitled *Going West* works across a variety of creative practice, including, film, music, animation, graphic design and photography.

The writer and illustrator Leanne Shapton, who grew up in Canada and is now based in New York, tests the boundaries of what a book can be in her work that is interdisciplinary in form. Her first novel *Important Artifacts and Personal Property from the Collection of Lenore Doolan and Harold Morris, Including Books, Street Fashion and Jewelry* (2009) describes a love affair in, texts and images, so that the story is told by a curator, instead of a narrator. Her book *Swimming Studies* described being a trainee Olympic swimmer, and is unconventional too, with its photographs of swimming costumes and sketches. Likewise her most recent work *Was She Pretty?* is a catalogue of ex-girlfriends. The inspiration for this work comes from staying at a boyfriend's house and seeing pictures of his ex-girlfriends everywhere in the house.

Another Canadian writer Sheila Heti has become a literary sensation in the United States with her experimental novel, which is ground breaking in form: *How Should a Person Be?* This fiction, chosen by the *New York Times* as one of the best books of 2012, is a book of constructed reality based on recorded interviews with her friends, although facts of their lives are altered; it is structured like a literary version of reality television. This is a genre-defying novel, a mash-up of memoir, fiction, emails, transcribed conversations, self-help and philosophy, with themes such as friendship, sex and love, and which asks important questions about young women's sexuality and their roles in late-capitalist society, whilst celebrating the power of female friendship.

What might have once been called vanity publishing has moved into the mainstream of the publishing industry. The bestseller *Fifty Shades of Grey*, which also explores female sexuality, began as a self-published work and also as a work of fan fiction, signifying a change in the relationship between readers and writers. The vanity publishing stigma has been lifted. Writers are now more at liberty to publish their own work, either online or in print, rather than being selected by agents and publishers to accept work that *they* deem worthy and saleable. And so, there is a real threat to traditional publishing houses, as more and more writers publish and promote their own work, as each day a new magazine, publishing company, website, blog or interactive forum springs up online.

Why is the realist novel in crisis?

There is a growing school of thought which believes that the realist novel is in crisis; this is the view of Professor of English David Shields, who resides at the University of Washington; he is the author of *The Thing About Life Is That One Day You'll Be Dead* and *Reality Hunger: A Manifesto*, an engaging work which presents the reader with a series of 617 alphabetically organized short provocations/statements/thoughts which encourage writers to produce work that is 'Nonlinear. Discontinuous. Collage-like' (p. 359) and to build work from scraps and embrace cross-formal experimentalism and plagiarism because 'The novel is dead. Long live the antinovel, built from scraps' (p. 327).

Shields suggests that here are a number of reasons why the realist novel is considered to be in crisis; for example, generic forms are exhausted, and too restricting. They do not reflect the complexities and subtleties of twenty-first-century life; they are too traditional, when traditions are changing. Realist novels are old-fashioned and stuck in the past. In this changing world where language is shifting and means of communications are constantly evolving, in particular social networking, Shields claims that it is time to create something new because realist novels are 'moribund', the reasons for this are 'they are ignoring the culture around them, where new, more exciting forms of narration and presentation and representation are being found (or rediscovered)' (D. Shields, *Reality Hunger: A Manifesto*, p. 262). Shields continues by saying, 'Conventional fiction teaches the reader that life is a coherent, fathomable whole that concludes in neatly wrapped-up revelation. Life, though ... channel surfing, trying to navigate the web ... flies at us in bright splinters' (p. 319).

Indeed, David Shields is not the only writer in recent years who has expressed dissatisfaction with the restrictions of realist fiction. British-born artist and writer Tom McCarthy, the author of fiction *Remainder and C*, who created the International Necronautical Society (INS) in 1999, which has led to installations and exhibitions in galleries and museums around the world, from Tate Britain and the ICA in London to The Drawing Center in New York, too feels that someone needs to challenge the realist novel. McCarthy, who frequently writes on literature and art for publications including the *London Review of Books*, *Artforum* and the *New York Times*, has the view that the experimental, the avant-garde should not be ignored, and to do so would be akin to ignoring Darwin.

However, in her essay *Two Paths for the Novel* (The New York Review of Books, 2008), Zadie Smith compares Tom McCarthy's novel *Remainder* with Joseph O'Neill's novel *Netherland*. She sees the two novels exemplifying competing strands in Western literature, the experimental *Remainder* and the realist *Netherland*. She argues that in healthy times the experimental and realist co-exist; however, currently times are not healthy and therefore the experimental novel maybe a fascination but it is a failure. In the light of McCarthy's experimental novel, *C*, being short listed for the Booker Prize in 2010, and *Tinkers* by Paul Harding, with its lack of plot, shifts in tenses, fragmentation and hallucinatory quality, winning the Pulitzer Prize, it appears that some critics disagree with her views.

As outlined, it appears that we are living through changing times, times in which *new* experimental fiction is being created. The following chapters will explore what twenty-first-century writers are doing that is considered *new*; it will also show how they are doing it, so that readers and writers of experimental fiction can understand what these works are doing and use the practices within their own work too.

Beyond Postmodernism

This chapter investigates writers who are moving away from fiction which privileges style over content, in favour of work that searches for meaning within their fiction, whilst exploring spirituality and *big* questions. As well as addressing the content of *beyond postmodernism* fiction, this chapter will outline some of the techniques writers use, so that experimental writers can practise these techniques and strategies too.

Why are some writers moving away from postmodernism?

In post-Millennium, post-Christian, post-9/11 times, there are a number of writers and readers who are moving away from fiction that is all surface no depth; the superficiality of some postmodern fiction is losing its power to entertain. These readers and writers are not satisfied by fiction which simply revels in playfully mixing forms and rewriting narratives; they no longer feel liberated by work which sees itself as a celebration from fixed truths and beliefs, nor do they delight in uncertainty. As Alex Grey makes the point in *The Mission of Art*: 'The current cultural situation is calling for individuals to transcend the fractured vision of postmodernism and awaken to some transpersonal and collective spiritual basis for truth and conscience' (p. 15). It is evident that a *new* fiction is evolving, one in which writers are searching for meaning through their work, and are asking philosophical questions about why we are here, in a world where meaning seems lost, or at the least ambiguous. This fiction invites the reader to be active and not a passive consumer, because the writers of such work are asking the reader to consider how they view the world and how they live their lives.

Why are some writers embracing spirituality?

The twenty-first century is an age in a state of flux. This is a period of enormous change, a change that has been identified in terms of changing cultural, political, economic and social trends. In addition, we have taken a quantum leap in our scientific and spiritual beliefs, questioning the way reality is constituted.

Religion, which comes from the Latin word 'religio', meaning to tie, to bind, is contested, and is seen as an incommensurate way of knowing, where truth is forever shifting. And so, religion has been going through something of a revolution, breaking free from formal structures, imposed by patriarchal institutions that have held it together for centuries. Although there is a rise in more fundamentalist religions, there is a decline in church-based practice; this, together with the breakdown of Grand Narratives, upheaval of paradigms, war, political unrest, the recession and angst about the meaninglessness of consumer and celebrity cultures, has resulted in 'other' belief systems emerging in recent years. Emancipation from religion transmitted through dogma, and living in a world where the division between *real* and virtual life is breaking down, the individual, which includes the writer, is free to create their own reality and life meaning.

It appears that ' … the dawn of the twenty-first century is unique in that the great religions and indigenous peoples of the world have grown beyond their former cultural isolation, and many great spiritual teachers have travelled throughout the world fostering a sense of interfaith fellowship … The Dalai Lama of Tibet is an exemplar … I believe deeply that we must find, all of us together, a new spirituality' (Alex Grey, p. 132). And it does seem that a new awareness may well be emerging, an expanding of consciousness; a consciousness that, it can be argued, has its roots in both the individual and the collective.

As a result, writers are emerging who are investigating this expanding consciousness and are embracing spirituality; they are searching for meaning through their fiction.

What is the content of New Era fiction?

The New Era fiction does not collude with postmodernism's abandonment with the search for meaning; nor does it embrace consumerism like many of the eighties and nineties writers explored in the postmodern section of this book. New Era fiction has a preoccupation with inner consciousness and examines the mind's interior, in some ways, not unlike the modernist writers. However, the New Era writers are provoking readers to look for a different kind of meaning, a meaning which may be said to be rejecting *old* values, those of religious doctrine. The New Era fiction is concerned with the writer's ideas and thoughts about spirituality. It can be argued that spirit (from the Latin 'spiritus' meaning breath, energy, force) motivates us to search for purpose in life, to enquire into our origins and identities, to endeavour to discover meaning and transcendence. Much can be said of the New Era writers, who create characters unlike the glamorous, passive, one-dimensional characters created by the Brat Pack writers. For example, the young British writer Grace McCleen in her novel *The Professor of Poetry* (2013) creates a very intense character: Elizabeth Stone. Professor Stones explores how 'the mind is brought into contact with the spiritual' (p. 222) and throughout the course of the book she engages in a passionate study of the works of T. S. Eliot and the music of poetry.

Some New Era fiction prompts its readers to reflect upon the world, and their place in it. It is work that is visionary and challenging. For example, *The Age of Miracles* by the American Karen Thompson Walker (2012) is a novel in which a giant earthquake knocks the Earth from its axis. The novel's theme is topical in the light of events in Japan; the massive earthquake that struck the country shifted the planet on its axis and shortened the Earth's day by a fraction of a second. In *The Age of Miracles*, however, a fiction narrated by a ten-year-old California girl, Julia, a quake shakes the planet causing the Earth's rotation to slow and days to lengthen, first by six minutes, then twelve minutes, then twenty-four. As the phenomenon, called *the slowing*, takes hold, days stretch to forty-eight hours, and gravity weakens. As a result, astronauts become stranded far from Earth and birds cease to fly.

The Age of Miracles netted a £500,000 publishing deal, almost unprecedented in such turbulent economic times. And Simon & Schuster fought off eight other publishers to land the deal. Suzanne Baboneau considered *The Age of Miracles* to be a novel of big ideas. She says, in a note to the reader at the beginning of the book: 'You are about to read a novel that we believe is very special indeed ... it is one of those rare novels that make us consider the way we look at the world, at how we structure our days and, beyond that, how easily the Earth could be knocked out of kilter and how our lives, as we know them, could alter forever ... '. Clearly, this fiction has depth and is not superficial in tone; far from it, it is fiction that is asking its readers to think, and consider issues that could *actually* happen, and what human beings might do in such circumstances. For example, what might characters do at 'the end of times'. Julia's friend, Hanna, is a Mormon, who had once told her that ' ... the church had pinpointed a certain square mile in Utah as the exact location of Jesus' next return to earth. They kept a giant grain silo there, she said, to feed the Mormons during the end times'. However, Julia's ' ... own family's religion was a bloodless breed of Lutheranism – we guarded no secrets, and we harboured no clear vision of the end of the world' (p. 25). It is therefore very poignant when Hanna and her family were preparing to leave for Utah:

> "Where are you going?" I asked.
>
> "Utah", Hanna said. She sounded scared.
>
> "When are you coming back?" I asked.
>
> "We're not"', she said.
>
> I felt a wave of panic. We'd spent so much time together that year that teachers sometimes called us by one another's name.

The British writer and academic Scarlett Thomas also creates characters who engage in debates about *big* ideas and pose *big* questions; for example, in *Our Tragic Universe*, she writes:

'But isn't the point of being alive to try to answer the big questions? I shook my head. For me it's about trying to work out what the questions are'. (Scarlett Thomas, Our Tragic Universe, Canongate, 2010, p. 400)

Sum Forty Tales from the Afterlives by the neuroscientist and writer David Eagleman is a collection of short stories which are concerned with the mystery of human existence, stories which ask questions such as: What happens to a person when they die? And what does it mean to be human? Undoubtedly death is a concept central to spiritual beliefs, one being explored by a number of writers in the twenty-first century, as Scarlett Thomas writes in *Our Tragic Universe*: 'Death has to be what defines life' (p. 209).

The work of British-born writer David Mitchell is interesting in that he employs some postmodern strategies, such as the use of interlocking narratives; for example, his (1999) novel *Ghostwritten* has nine intersecting narratives. His work *Number9dream* (2001) interweaves narratives and uses cultural signifiers, John Lennon, for example. However, this work illustrates the desire human beings have to create meaning in their lives and to have something to believe in. *Number9dream* is set in Japan; it is Eiji Miyake's search for the father he's never met. Told in the first person by nineteen-year-old Eiji as he approaches his twentieth birthday, this fiction breaks convention by juxtaposing Eiji's imaginative journey towards identity through Tokyo's postmodern underworld, that is, video arcades, computer games and films, a plurality of realities, with his journey to find his father, a journey which represents the human desire to have meaning in life. Eiji is searching for meaning in a postmodern, late-capitalist society where there appears to be no meaning, but he has discovered a meaning, to find his father.

The content of New Era fiction is often suffused with spirituality, for example, *The Unlikely Pilgrimage of Harold Fry* by Rachel Joyce. This fiction, although conventional in form, that is, it follows the structure of a quest plot, ponders upon *big* questions. The protagonist, Harold Fry, walks from one end of Britain to the other, meeting a variety of characters along the way and he learns a variety of lessons from each character that he meets. The key to the novel appears to be discovered in the epigraph, at the beginning of the text, which quotes John Bunyan's *The Pilgrim's Progress*: '... His first avowed intent To be a pilgrim'. Harold does not believe in God, although he can be viewed as the contemporary equivalent of Bunyan's Christian. He is walking to atone for the mistakes he has made in his life, and to reflect upon his life in the face of death, that is, the imminent death of a former colleague, Queenie Hennessy. 'He understood that in walking to atone for the mistakes he had made, it was also his journey to accept the strangeness of others' (p. 87).

Experiment with this: Learning to Write Reflectively

Create a character embarking on a pilgrimage. Who are they? What is the catalyst for them embarking on a pilgrimage? Where are they starting from and where are they going to? Describe the pilgrimage and the characters the protagonist meets on the way: allow the protagonist to 'accept the strangeness of others', and to reflect upon their life and the mistakes they have made.

All Is Song by Samantha Harvey is another fiction which poses many thought-provoking questions, inviting the reader to reflect upon such issues as: 'What is love? – Is it beauty? Is it spirituality?' (p. 95). In addition, there is considerable debate throughout the narrative upon the nature of belief: 'Pa asked me ... what the nature of your faith was ... I said you believed in a supreme being' (pp. 62–3). Also, the anxieties and 'enormous unrest in the world ... Every age has its unrest ... but this one more so ...' (pp. 70–1). Michael Symmons Roberts debates ethical questions in his fiction *Breath*, a narrative which is a meditation on the nature of forgiveness, duty, absolution and faith.

And Scarlett Thomas reflects upon belief systems in *Our Tragic Universe*: 'In Taoism, it's only nothingness that gives anything meaning' (p. 151). Likewise, Nicole Krauss, in *Man Walks into a Room*: 'The Bible, yes. Do you like it? ... I'm starving for glory ... My head was full of all this Hindu stuff, which was all well and good, except I hadn't thought about Jesus since I was a kid and my Sunday school teacher told me Jesus was my only true friend' (pp. 198–9).

The Zen Buddhist priest, award-winning novelist and film maker, Ruth Ozeki, who was born and raised in Connecticut by an American father and a Japanese mother, explores spirituality in her fiction *A Tale for the Time Being*, a narrative about the ways in which reading and writing connect people who will never meet: Nao, a school girl from Tokyo, and Ruth, a woman who lives in British Columbia. As a result of a tsunami, Nao's diary is washed ashore in a *Hello Kitty* lunch box and Ruth finds it. This rich and complex fiction is a meditation on Zen philosophy, environmental issues, time, memory and quantum physics, a fiction inscribed with Japanese writing, different fonts, footnotes and a cross pollination of cultures. Part 1 opens with, 'For The Time Being', the eleventh chapter of *The Treasury of the True Dharma Eye* by the author and Japanese master Dogen Zenji. Throughout the narrative, the reader is invited to contemplate on the nature of human conscience, what it means to philosophize and to study the self.

Experiment with this: Learning to Explore *Big* Questions Through Fiction

Imagine a character who is at a cross roads in their life. Through dialogue and interior monologue write a section from a novel in which they debate big questions; choose one, two or all of these: what is the nature of self/beauty/truth/death/faith? Also have the character reflecting upon the twenty-first century and their place in it.

In addition to debating big questions, New Era fiction can also be seen to be questioning postmodern culture; Scarlett Thomas, in particular, does this. As Meg says, 'I hate celebrity culture; it's just another form of clichéd narrative entertainment' (Our Tragic Universe, p. 104). Later, in the novel: 'unless we gave up on ... twenty four hour drama and entertainment, we were in danger of turning ourselves into fictional characters with no use beyond entertaining people ... We would become little more than character arcs, with nothing in our lives apart from getting to act, two and then act three and the dying' (Our Tragic, pp. 336–7).

What is the form of New Era fiction?

Some of the form of New Era fiction is traditional, for example, as already mentioned, *The Unlikely Pilgrimage of Harold Fry*. The fiction of Scarlett Thomas is also traditional realist in form, a narrative with a beginning, middle and end, but with the characters dropping in and out of deep philosophical discussion about our tragic universe.

However, the form of *Sum* by David Eagleman may be described as very short stories where each piece tells a completely different version of the afterlife. There is a message behind the stories, which is: we don't know whether there is an afterlife or not. These stories can be said to be more philosophical debates than actual fiction; for example, *Adhesion* reads: 'Our life on Earth represents an experiment in which they are trying to figure out what makes people stick together' (p. 34) and *Conservation*: 'What we have deduced about the Big Bang is almost exactly wrong' (p. 84). The fiction is often told in second-person point of view in spare, factual language.

Experiment with this: Learning to Experiment with Form

Using a second-person point of view, write a very short piece, using stark, scientific language, on afterlife. Have a message behind the fiction, which is: we don't know, the afterlife cannot be proven.

The History of Love by Nicole Krauss has been described as a complex Russian-doll structure; a narrative inside another inside another. The form is fragmented. There are multiple voices, multiple narrative strands set out on the page in blocks of text; for example, graphics are also used throughout the fiction (p. 196). The form, therefore, is not dissimilar to postmodern fictions, that is, self reflexive and fragmented. However, the content of the work is *all depth*. Krauss meditates upon war, loneliness, death and human resilience. Likewise her novel *Man Walks into a Room* is an engaging narrative as well as a philosophical read: 'What if we defined the spiritual aspect of human nature as the need to belong – be it at some cosmological, biological, or social level. What people call spiritual experiences usually involve a sudden feeling of being supernaturally connected in some way, right?' (p. 104).

The Shock of the Fall by Nathan Filer, which explores the mental health issues of his protagonist, Matthew, also has a complex narrative structure and experiments with graphics and fonts. In addition to writing his family's story within the book, Matthew also draws a family portrait which conveys this Russian-doll narrative structure:

> I took one of the framed pictures of Simon from the mantelpiece – the one of him beaming proudly in his new school uniform – and drew it on the little table beside the couch, where we kept the newspapers. I drew Mum beside him, then myself between her and Dad ... Self-portraits are the hardest. It's hard to capture your own self, or even know what it is. In the end I decided to do myself with a sketchbook on my knees, drawing a picture. And if you look carefully, you can make out the top of the picture – and it's the one we're in.
>
> I think that's sort of what I'm doing now too. I am writing myself into my own story, and I am telling it from within. (p. 199)

The content of this work is all depth, too; it insightfully explores the bond of a family and the impact the death of Simon has on each family member, in particular his brother, Matthew.

Experiment with this: Learning to Use a Russian-Doll Narrative Structure, that is, One Narrative Inside Another, Inside Another

Use the theme Love. Experiment with multiple narrative, multiple voices and fragmentation. Allow the multiple voices to debate the theme of love; focus on the voices' spiritual development which evolves as a result of the debate.

Changing Perceptions of Reality

This chapter explores the ways in which our beliefs about reality are being challenged as boundaries of art, reality, social networking, celebrity, advertising, marketing and publicity are becoming increasingly blurred, so that the experimental reader can understand how these boundaries are being challenged and the writer can experiment with techniques that enable them to do this too.

What is real in the twenty-first century?

When writing about how the real is viewed in the twenty-first century, Professor David Shields writes in *Reality Hunger: A Manifesto*: 'We seek new means of creating the real' (p. 54). These new means of creating the real appears to be linked to a more conscious manipulation of the real and truth, concepts relevant to social networking, which inspired Lottie Moggach to write her debut novel *Kiss Me First*. The book explores how social networking is affecting our sense of reality, truth, identity and our connections with others and shows that virtual relationships are based on blurring reality. Online, people have the opportunity to present unreal images of themselves, so that they can be seen as they would like to be seen, rather than how they actually are, and friends often accept these images without question. Therefore, anything posted could be a lie, even the fact that someone existed at all; this is the premise of the novel. Tess wants to commit suicide without her family and friends knowing she has gone, and so she hires Leila to take over her virtual life following her death, assuming her identity, answering emails, operating her Facebook page, and she does, until the cracks between real and virtual lives appear.

Experiment with this: Learning to Manipulate the Real

Write a scene from a novel in which a protagonist manipulates 'friends' by presenting unreal facts, images and stories online. Write a second scene where the protagonist is seen in the real world as they actually are, rather than how they want to be seen.

Manipulating the truth and reality can also be the means by which an author creates an image in order to sell a product, a book, for example, *Sarah* by J. T. Le Roy. *Sarah* is an *autobiographical* narrative written by Mr J. T. Le Roy (Jeremiah 'Terminator' Le Roy). This *fiction* is about life as a truck-stop prostitute in California, told by a 12-year-old boy, nicknamed, Cherry Vanilla, who aspired to be a girl.

The controversial subject matter in Le Roy's work created interest and various journalists sought out *his* identity. Le Roy, claiming to be shy, appeared in public in blonde wig, big shades, hat, protected by *his* family, claiming they were there to protect him from temptations of his former life as a drug addict. However, an article in *New York* magazine, by Stephen Beachy, in October 2005, raised the possibility that Mr Le Roy didn't exist and suggested that Ms Laura Albert might be the author, saying that he felt the 'hoax' was a promotional device. Ms Albert later confirmed this, claiming that Mr Le Roy was a 'veil' and not a 'hoax'. By writing as Le Roy, she was able to write things she could not have done as Laura Albert. However, the work being passed off as autobiography was clearly a fiction. A media frenzy ensued as Mr J. T. Le Roy's readers came to terms with the fact that they had been duped by an elaborate literary hoax.

In January 2006, *The Times* named the person who had appeared in disguise as Mr Le Roy was, in fact, Savannah Knoop, the half-sister of Ms Albert's partner, Geoffrey Knoop. In July 2007, *Antidote International Films*, which had bought the rights to adapt 'Sarah', sued

Ms Albert for fraud; she had signed documents as J. T. Le Roy. She was ordered to pay $350,000 in legal fees. The trial, covered by Alan Feuer, for the *Times*, was: 'an oddly highbrow exploration of a psyche-literary landscape filled with references to the imagination's fungible relation to reality and the bond that exists between the writer and the work'. In 2008, Savannah Knoop published *Girl Boy Girl: How I Became JT LeRoy*, a memoir about her years spent as Le Roy.

The Le Roy case has been compared with that of James Frey author of the memoir *A Million Little Pieces*. In January 2008, the *Smoking Gun* website published an article alleging that Frey fabricated large parts of his memoir. There was one incident, in particular. This was in 1986, when a car-train crash took place in Michigan, while Frey was high on crack; he was imprisoned. After initial support from his publishers, and Oprah Winfrey, who defended Frey on TV, facts later emerged that the incident had been altered and embellished. Later, on Winfrey's TV show, Frey admitted he *lied* to her; in fact he had spent a few hours in jail, not the 87 days that he had claimed in his memoir. Frey concluded that he was writing about a character he'd created in his mind to help him cope with his addiction, a character more aggressive than the 'real' him. This too provoked a media frenzy.

In *Reality Hunger: A Manifesto*, David Shields enters the memoir debate: 'How can we enjoy memoirs, believing them to be true, when nothing, as everyone knows, is so unreliable as memory?...We remember what suits us, and there's no limit to what we can forget' (p. 25). '...memoirs really can claim to be modern novels, all the way down to the presence of an unreliable narrator' (pp. 25–6). In terms of the Frey case, he writes, 'I'm disappointed not that Frey is a liar but that he isn't a better one. He should have said, *Everyone who writes about himself is a liar. I created a person meaner, funnier, more filled with life than I could ever be*' (p. 43). But surely his most interesting point, which can be attributed to the Frey and Le Roy case, is that 'Capitalism implies and induces insecurity, which is constantly being exploited, of course, by all sorts of people selling things' (p. 44). Of course, this includes the sale of books, but should readers' insecurities be manipulated?

Should readers be exploited and duped by literary hoaxes? Should the *real* person who has written the book be named as the *real* author on the cover? If a reader is told they are reading a memoir, should they expect the work to be *true*? But in the twenty-first century, when our beliefs about truth and reality are constantly shifting, do we know what is true or real anymore? Is it inevitable that the boundaries of art, reality, advertising, marketing and publicity will become increasingly blurred in a consumer society? Hasn't the market already become the *real* reality for many consumers? Without doubt, there are a number of ethical issues and implications for both the reader and writer of fiction that need to be addressed.

Experiment with this: Learning to Debate the Real Using Dialogue

Write an extract from a novel in which two characters disagree about what they consider to be real. Use dialogue to reveal their beliefs.

To return to memoir, may be David Shields has a point when he says that when writing memoir the writer is simply using 'the nuts and bolts of your own life to illustrate your vision. It isn't really me; it's a character based on myself that I made up in order to illustrate things I want to say...memoir is as far from real life as fiction is' (p. 39). It is simply the duty of the writer to persuade the reader that the 'narrator is trying, as honestly as possible, to get to the bottom of the experience at hand' (p. 40). So, has Shields a point? Is truth achieved not through the re-telling of *real* events, but when 'the reader comes to believe that the writer is working hard to engage with the experience at hand?' Is it the case that, what *really* happened to the writer isn't what matters? 'What matters is the larger sense that the writer is able to make of what happened'. And for this, as Shields claims: 'For that the power of the imagination is required' (pp. 41–2).

Experiment with this: Learning to Use the Power of the Imagination

Under the guise of memoir, write about an experience that did not *actually* happen but write about it in such a way as to persuade the reader that it did in order to 'get to the bottom of the experience at hand'.

Experiment with this: Learning to Use Writing Bursts

Choose ONE of the following writing bursts and continue the story:

(1) The figure in this scene is a version of myself or at least someone I used to be...
(2) I remember bits and pieces...
(3) This was what I was told... but I remember it like this...

Anti-Novels Built from Scraps

This chapter will enable readers of experimental fiction to understand genre-defying work which is ground breaking in form and it will give writers the opportunity to experiment with these two practices.

Which writers are building their fictions from scraps?

In the twenty-first century there are a number of writers who are experimenting by building their fictions from scraps of different discourses, for example, Mark Z. Danielewski, in his experimental work, *House of Leaves* (2000). In this fiction Danielewski experiments with layout and form, and in so doing, he pushes back the boundaries of what fiction can be. This kind of fiction has been referred to as ergodic literature, a term derived from the Greek words *ergon*, meaning work, and *hodos*, meaning path. *House of Leaves* is a labyrinth of a book, crammed with minutiae: copious footnotes, many of which contain further footnotes, some referencing books that do not exist. There are also appendix, poems, letters, scripts and multiple narrators who interact with each other throughout the narrative.

The Selected Works of T. S. Spivet by Reif Larsen (2009) is another fiction which breaks the boundaries of traditional narrative form by using other media which challenges the physicality of the book. The text includes drawings purported to be done by Spivet which have *actually* been created by Larsen and passed to his friend, the artist, Ben Gibson, who re-drafted and completed them. The plot line is illustrated with images which further the narrative by providing charts, lists, sketches and maps, which illustrate the 12-year-old Spivet's interest with cartography.

Experiment with this: Learning to Build Fiction from Scraps in a Non-linear Form

Using multiple discourses, choose from any of the following: recipes, graffiti, literary theory, emails, poetry, text messages, lists, lyrics, autobiography. Experiment with a fiction which has the title: The Weird World of Walter Woolf

---

Rob Ryan is a Spanish writer and visual artist who specializes in paper cutting, screen printing, drawing and painting. In his works *This Is For You* (2007) and *A Sky Full of Kindness* (2011), all the illustrations are paper cut-outs, even the prose-poetry text, which is integrated into the pictures, is cut out from a single sheet of paper. The cut-outs are photographed on white paper so that shadows on the text are part of the design.

In her fiction, *Like Bees to Honey*, Caroline Smailes experiments with scraps of text and fonts and layout. There is a lyrical, philosophical, spiritual tone to Nina's narrative. In this work, the unstable heroine returns to her homeland Malta with her son, Christopher, leaving her husband, Matt, and other child, Molly, in England. Malta is a meeting place for restless souls who have not yet completed their transition to paradise. There are sections within the work devoted to individual souls; the paper of these is edged in black – like memorial cards.

Black Boxes is another fiction by Smailes which breaks with traditional realism. Ana Lewis has two children: Pip, who writes a diary, and Davie. Ana has taken an overdose. *Black Boxes* follows her final hours as the pills kick in and the reader becomes aware of the sequence of events that brought about this moment. The narrative is told within the context of two black boxes, one Ana's, one Pip's. As Ana demands silence, Pip and Davie communicate through finger sign language and the text is integrated with this communication in graphics.

Audrey Niffenegger, author of the *Time Traveller's Wife*, also created a fiction, *Incestuous Sisters*. She calls the books she makes 'visual novels' as she 'loves them as objects' also to 'acknowledge a debt to Lynd Ward', whose 'woodcut novel *God's Man* was the first book of this kind I ever saw, and to differentiate my books from graphic novels' (Afterword *Incestuous Sisters*). The images and text tell the story. The images are aquatints. Aquatint is an antique process. The images are 'made by covering a zinc plate with an acid-resistant ground, drawing through the ground with a needle, and immersing the plate in a nitric acid bath, which results in a plate that has the lines of the drawing etched into it. To create tone, fine rosin dust is melted onto the plate. I block out areas that should not be bitten by the acid, and the plate is placed in the acid bath in successive stages. I am working in reverse, blind; I don't know what's actually on the plate until I print it. The colour is watercolour, painted onto each print'.

Incestuous Sisters took fourteen years to complete. Niffenegger was working on *The Time Traveller's Wife* at the same time. She says that when she is explaining the fiction to a reader who hasn't yet seen the book that they must 'image a silent film made from Japanese prints, a melodrama of sibling rivalry, a silent opera hat features women with very long hair and a flying green boy. I never try to explain what it means; you can find that out for yourself' (Afterword *Incestuous Sisters*).

Experiment with this: Learning to Experiment with Fiction That Uses More than Words

Using the title 'A Story of Scraps' create a fiction which incorporates sketches, footnotes, maps, and images and experiments with typography to challenge the boundaries of traditional narrative form and the physicality of the book.

How are other writers challenging traditional realist fiction?

Senior lecturer in Creative Writing at Manchester Metropolitan, Manchester campus, Nicholas Royle, who runs *Nightjar Press*, reviews fiction for the *Independent* and is the author of the novels *The Director's Cut*, *Antwerp* and short-story collection *Mortality*. He has experimented with metafiction, taking it to its extreme in his novel *First Novel*. There are stories within stories within stories, as it says in the novel, 'Everything is either or, and inside each either or is another either or, like Russian dolls' (p. 265). Indeed, the novel has a complex form. The author of one of the narratives is a Creative Writing tutor and other narratives are written by the tutor's students; it transpires that the students become the protagonists of their own narratives, which begs the questions: are the writers writing memoir or fiction? The novel also provokes the reader to ask: What is fact and what is fiction? Real events and real people – for example, the case of Dr Harold Shipman – are weaved into the narrative; likewise, a number of real writers, for example, Siri Hustvedt, appear in the novel.

Professor of English at the University of Sussex Nicholas Royle, too, writes an engaging Afterword: Reality Fiction, in his experimental work *Quilt*. In this Afterword, Royle reflects on the process of writing and asks: 'Is the author of the afterword simply the *same* as the author of the novel?' (p. 152). He goes on to say that 'The novel is a space of play' (p. 152). And yet the novel '…faces challenges and pressures unimaginable in earlier times' (p. 153). He ponders on how a novel should 'deal with the reality of telephones and other, newer modes of telecommunication?' (p. 156). And he inscribes the beginning of his fiction into the Afterword: 'You recall the beginning: 'In the middle of the night the phone rings, over and over, but I don't hear it'. He writes, 'The reader hears about what the narrator doesn't hear. It is the novel calling. The novel is a kind of weird telephone exchange'. Further complexity is added when Royle informs the reader that 'Reality literature would be writing that acknowledges this weirdness and goes somewhere that was not foreseeable, either for the author or the reader'.

It is explicit that Royle is exploring the notion of reality, saying that '…reality literature is the first literary genre to be explicitly derived from TV' (p. 157), although he tells the reader that it needs to be acknowledged that 'Reality TV is of course a fiction' (p. 158) and that reality literature '…seeks to question and complicate, to dislocate and interfere' (p. 158), as *Quilt* does. Royle invites the reader to question, 'Is it a literary reality or a literature of reality?' and he tells the reader that 'To read a novel is to enter a world of magical thinking' (p. 158). Royle has certainly created 'a magical world of thinking' in his novel *Quilt*, which is also a 'space of quilted thinking' (p. 159), that is, a complex space of play and inventiveness where there are '…layers and pockets of voices, feelings, thoughts' (p. 159).

Quilt is a highly original and experimental work which asks the reader to consider: What is a reader? What is a writer? By reading *Quilt*, the reader becomes an active producer of meaning of the text and the writer is invited to consider new ways of writing fictions.

In addition to writers who are taking metafiction to thought-provoking extremes, there are also a number of writers who embrace cross-formal experimentation in their pursuit of experimentation. In his work, *Someone Called Derrida*, John Schad blurs genres and discourses and brings together literary theory and creative writing. *Someone Called Derrida* is a non-linear work which splices *true* stories inherited from Schad's own father, a minister of religion, and the *true* stories from father of deconstruction, Jacques Derrida. Schad says, in a note at the beginning of the book: 'This book is an experiment in which I am often attempting a style that is, in many ways, novelistic; however, I am also attempting that equally difficult thing-to tell the truth'.

Artful by Ali Smith is a book that defies categorization; it is fiction and non-fiction, literary criticism and essay, a kind of *Room of One's Own* for twenty-first-century writers and readers of experimental fiction. A text built from scraps, it explores what writing can do and what writing can mean. *Artful* is a book of ideas narrated by a character who is literally haunted by her former lover, the writer of a series of lectures about literature and art. Indeed, the sections of the book, *On time, On form, On edge* and *On offer and on reflection*, are adapted from four lectures given by Ali Smith at Oxford University. At the back of the book, there are a number of drawings and photographs that have informed the text, likewise a list of text permissions from works that have been weaved into *Artful*.

Lila Azam Zanganeh's work, *The Enchanter: Nabokov and Happiness*, might be described as a playful, semi-fictionalized sequence of elaborations – or variations – on the experience of being a passionate Nabokov reader. There is no linear narrative. Instead, Zanganeh invents an interview with Nabokov and portrays a series of encounters with moments from his biography; the result is a fiction which is both serious and playful, one that experiments with genres, discourses and boundaries and contains elements of memoir, biography and criticism.

Experiment with this: Learning to *Play* Within Fiction and to Splice *Real* Stories about *Real* People and to Experiment with Metafiction

Choose a *real* character from history, for example, William Shakespeare; splice *true* stories from Shakespeare's life with fictions from your own life as a writer, create a short story that experiments with fact and fiction, a text that is both playful and serious, one that questions the role of the reader and the writer.

Electronic/Hyper/Interactive Fiction

There are a number of writers who are currently trying to find new ways of telling stories, ways that will stretch the form to its limits. The printed book is no longer the defining literary format; this is having an impact on writers and readers, which is leading to new approaches to reading and writing fiction. To offer the reader an insight into this shift, this chapter explores these changes and also the developments taking place in the publishing industry. In addition, these are here suggesting as to how the contemporary writer can experiment with these practices.

How is the publishing industry changing?

Without doubt, print is dying and digital is surging. Consequently, this acceleration of technology is impacting upon the writer and reader, influencing the ways in which fiction can be constructed and read. Indeed, the rise of digital technology and ebooks and the decline of traditional print media and of high-street retailers, as more and more readers purchase books online, are challenging the structure of creating, buying and selling books; therefore, a very competitive market is now being established.

With a series of classic titles, for example, *The Thirty Nine Steps* by John Buchan, to be released in an interactive format, the publishing companies Harper Collins and Faber are now encouraging contemporary writers to get together with software developers to produce experimental works.

In addition, opportunities for self-promoting and self-publishing are increasing; for example, *How to Publish Your Own ebook* is just one of a number of books that can be bought to encourage and support this process.

Some writers, readers and certainly publishers, whose businesses are seriously threatened by this paradigm shift, view this as cause for concern. The writer Jonathan Franzen, for example, believes readers are becoming shallow, less able to concentrate on the deeper meaning of books. In the age of shortening attention spans, the kernel of books can be expressed in much shorter forms. And yet, with the vast potential of the Web – quick hits, social network sites, twitter, blogs and online forums – readers have swifter access to fiction and new mediums and genres are emerging as writers are free to experiment in a very different space than that of the page.

Writers are developing their creativity in ways they choose and not necessarily to fall in line with publishing trends dictated to by the big publishing houses. Writers are making their own trends, and in so doing, they are discovering new ways of self-expression, new techniques, new strategies, new ways of communicating their new ideas and ultimately are having more control over their work.

What are the advantages of ebooks?

As ebooks can be downloaded and are cheaper to produce, they accounted for 10 per cent of sales in 2011 and 30 per cent of sales in 2012; this is a massive transition, similar to what took place in the music industry 10 years ago.

Fifty Shades of Grey by E. L. James, an erotic fiction, has risen to the top of ebooks sales in the United States. This book was originally launched online by the virtual publisher *Writer's Coffee Shop*; it was the first book to sell more than a million copies on Kindle. This illustrates that anyone can write on the internet, promote their work, build up a following and be downloaded on to Kobos and Kindles. When *Fifty Shades of Grey* went into print, it sold more than any previous novel. In June 2012, in Britain, 200,000 copies a week were sold and 15 million copies had been sold in the United States and Canada; it is set to overtake Dan Brown's *The Da Vinci Code* and the Harry Potter books as the bestselling paperback book ever, with follow-ups: *Fifty Shades Darker* and *Fifty Shades Freed*. The film rights have been sold for 3.2 million and a licensing agent appointed to handle all the spin-offs, for example, jewellery, perfume and lipstick. Likewise, teenager Beth Reekles originally posted her novel *Kissing Booth* on the site Wattpad, an online community themed around writing and story-telling; consequently, it was published as an ebook by Random House in December 2012 and in paperback in 2013. It appears that the power of the internet cannot be underestimated; cyberscouts now frequently scour the Web for undiscovered talent.

However, the writer Julian Barnes thinks that the ebook will never supplant the physical book as every book feels and looks different, whereas every Kindle download feels and looks exactly the same. However, he suggests that the ereader will one day be able to click a smell function to make, for example, a Dickens novel suddenly reek of damp paper and nicotine, like old books discovered in second-hand shops. Victoria Barnsley, head of Harper Collins, has made the point that in the twenty-first century publishers can't see themselves as simply book publishers, and instead, they need to view themselves as multimedia content producers.

Is Twitter the future of fiction?

Jennifer Egan, author of *A Visit from the Goon Squad*, which won the Pulitzer Prize, 2001, used innovative methods to tell a story, with chapters being written like PowerPoint slides and celebrity interviews. She experimented in 2012 with her work *Black Box*, a fiction about a futuristic female spy and her mission as recorded in her log. Originally Egan wrote the story by hand in a notebook with eight black-outlined rectangle spaces on each page. However, she revealed this fiction one tweet at a time at @NYerFiction between 8.00 p.m. and 9.00 p.m. from 24 May 2012 for ten days, attracted by the intimacy and interconnectednss of reaching readers through their phones.

Using his website, metamorphiction.com, Jeff Noon has developed his work to include electronic versions of his previous work. He is engaging in collaborative projects with musicians and other writers and also using Twitter to put out 140-character fictions he refers to as 'microspores'. Ideas that he once recorded since the 1980s in notebooks are now being featured online. He is also producing online poetry, and a project he refers to as 'Electronic Nocturne' considers what post-digital culture might look like; what will come after now?

In October 2012, *The Guardian* challenged some well-known writers to come up with a story of up to 140 characters; Ian Rankin and S. J. Watson were two writers who rose to the challenge.

Experiment with this: Learning to Write Twitter Fiction

Experiment with fiction. Then experiment with writing a complete story of your own, of up to 140 characters.

Caroline Smailes's *99 Reasons Why* published by the Friday Project, according to its website 'the experimental imprint of Harper Collins', has nine possible outcomes to Kate's story which the reader can navigate through an ereading device; each outcome is different and exposes a little more of Kate's world. An additional ending is given online and the eleventh ending will be auctioned for charity. In a radical departure from literary tradition, *99 Reasons Why* has a choice of 11 possible endings (log on to http://www.carolinesmailes.co.uk). This digital fiction gives the reader greater autonomy over the text and encourages them to be engaged, interactive readers, leading some critics to voice concerns that more and more authority is now lying with the reader as opposed to the writer, taking Barthes' polemic, 'death of the author, birth of the reader', to its ultimate conclusion.

Experiment with this: Learning to Create an Interactive Fiction

Write a short story using the title 'It's Your Choice'. Write four possible outcomes to the story. Post the story online and ask readers to select their favourite outcome.

Further Reading

Atkinson, Kate (2013) Life after Life, London: Doubleday.

Eagleman, David (2009) Sum, Edinburgh: Canongate.

Filer, Nathan (2013) The Shock of the Fall, London: Harper Collins.

Frey, James (2003) A Million Little Pieces, London: John Murray.

Grey, Alex (1998) The Mission of Art, London: Shambhala Publications.

Harding, Paul (2010) Tinkers, London: William Heinemann.

Harvey, Samantha (2012) All Is Song, London: Jonathan Cape.

Heti, Shelia (2013) How Should a Person Be? London: Harvill Secker.

Joyce, Rachel (2012) The Unlikely Pilgrimage of Harold Fry, London: Doubleday.

Krauss, Nicole (2002) Man Walks into a Room: London: Penguin Books.

—— (2005) The History of Love, London: Penguin Books.

—— (2010) Great House, London: Penguin Books.

Larsen, Reif (2010) The Selected Works of Spivet, T. S., London: Vintage.

Le Roy, J. T. (2000) Sarah, London: Bloomsbury.

Martel, Yann (2002) The Life of Pi, Edinburgh: Canongate.

—— (2011) Beatrice and Virgil, Edinburgh: Canongate.

McCarthy, Tom (2010) C, London: Jonathan Cape.

McCleen, Grace (2013) The Professor of Poetry, London: Sceptre.

Mitchell, David (2001) Number9dream, London: Sceptre.

Moggach, Lottie (2013) Kiss Me First, London: Picador.

Niffenegger, Audrey (2005) The Incestuous Sisters, London: Jonathan Cape.

Ozeki, Ruth (2013) A Tale for the Time Being, Edinburgh: Canongate.

Roberts Symmons, Michael (2009) Breath, London: Vintage.

Royle, Nicholas (2010) Quilt, Brighton: Myriad Editions.

—— (2013) First Novel, London: Jonathan Cape.

Ryan, Rob (2010) A Sky Full of Kindness, London: Sceptre.

Schad, John (2007) Someone Called Derrida, Eastbourne: Sussex Academic Press.

Shields, David (2010) Reality Hunger, London: Hamish Hamilton.

Smailes, Caroline (2012) 99 Reasons Why, London: The Friday Project.

Thomas, Scarlett (2011) Our Tragic Universe, Edinburgh: Canongate.

Walker Thompson, Karen (2013) Age of Miracles, London: Simon & Schuster.

Winterson, Jeanette (1996) Art Objects, London: Vintage.

Conclusion

How can writers engage in experimental writing practice?

It can be said that some writers do set out to be experimental for a variety of reasons, outlined in the introduction of this book. And this experimentation can be done in a variety of ways, shown in the creative writing exercises throughout this book, but they are tried and tested ways. So, what counts as experimental these days? And how can it be achieved?

Notions of experimental or avant garde have always been problematic. And yet, throughout history, writers have engaged with experimentation, often as a means of interacting with the times in which they are living. In the twenty-first century, this is still the case, but how can and how are writers doing this? Writers, especially those working in universities, studying on postgraduate programmes are engaging with praxis, that is, creative writing as research.

What are the implications for the writer wishing to experiment?

By engaging in experimentation, writers are taking the risk of being marginalized by readers, who judge work by the aesthetic standards that the writer has rejected or abandoned. This may lead to problems for writers wanting to be published by mainstream publishers, who want to make a profit and are loathe to take risks in such difficult economic times through the publishing of new work that may only attract a small readership, and therefore no profit. And yet, with the success of *C* and *Tinkers*, it appears that it can pay to take risks. However, fundamentally, it seems that Britain, in particular, has lost its risk-taking culture; publishing, it can be argued, is paying too much attention to pleasing readers, even though readers are being starved of fresh writing talent by a very real emphasis on commercial success by cash-strapped publishing houses. So, what are the answers to these dilemmas?

With access to the net, writers and readers have never been in a better position to communicate with other readers and writers. Although not in a traditional sense, writers are still able to showcase their work and reach an audience online. It is a question of thinking outside the box, or off the paper page. Self-promoting work is now an acceptable way of reaching readers and being true to the writer's integrity, and, in some cases, it is being seen as a very real threat to publishing houses. It is worth considering: Why should mainstream publishers have the monopoly on choosing work that they deem suitable for a readership if that means that a considerable amount of fresh, exciting, worthwhile fiction is never going to be read? Isn't it true that some fiction rejected in one time is then revered in another? Isn't it a question of the writer having faith in their work, and being true to their own artistic ideals? Considering the implications for the writer wishing to experiment in time, why is it still necessary for the writer to experiment?

Can this contradictory, complex world be represented by traditional-realist fiction?

This fast-paced, multi-narrative, multi-voiced world cannot be represented by simplistic, realist fiction. Writers need to reflect upon the speed of the twenty-first century, which is difficult if they are bound by plot. The linear narrative – beginning, middle, ending – does not ring true anymore. And so it is time for writers and readers to develop a spirit of adventure and make different journeys with different fictions to map the way. These different narratives are already emerging. As the Australian writer Gail Jones suggests, contemporary technologies are changing the ways in which stories are told and the ways in which experience is imagined.

As David Shield's writes, 'Facts quicken, multiply, change shape, elude us and bombard our lives with increasingly suspicious promises,' so that we are 'no longer able to depend on canonical literature,' as we 'journey increasingly across boundaries, along borders, into fringes, and finally through our yearnings to quest, where only more questions are found' (p. 79). Indeed, it is time to create fictions that at least engage with such questions; it is time to challenge orthodoxy and narrative, to push work to a more exciting realm, not ape what has gone before, nostalgically recreating *old* fiction for a *new* generation. Surely writers and readers deserve more? Ben Marcus, author of a collection of experimental short stories *The Age of Wire and String* and *The Flame Alphabet*, which has been referred to as an anti-narrative, is of the same opinion. Reacting to points made by Jonathan Franzen that experimental fiction was damaging the future of literature and scaring off potential readers, Marcus fought back by saying that he considered experimentation to be healthy, and that writers should be pushing linguistic barriers and making new pathways. Twice named Granta's best British young writer, and author of *Politics* (2003) and *The Escape* (2009), Adam Thirlwell also believes in the value of experimental fiction. The American novelist and short story writer, and author of *The Virgin Suicides* (1993), Jeffrey Eugenides agrees, acknowledging the need to describe something new about human experience or consciousness, which is what he considers to be the drive behind literary innovation.

The new era is about creating something new and fresh to capture the spirit of the twenty-first century. If writing does not evolve, it will be stale, dull, unadventurous. Alex Clark, a contributor to the *Observer* and former Booker Prize judge, has stated that writing should not be about producing something safe, it should be about producing something which unsettles, disturbs even. Certainly, writing should make readers think, question, challenge assumptions, unsettle, re-define, grow and not stay stuck in the past on a treadmill of repetition, of being in a comfort zone, with no surprises, no shocks, no new adventures. Fiction has to evolve. 'If fiction is to have any future in the technological dream/nightmare of the twenty first century it needs, more than ever, to remember itself as imaginative, innovative, Other' (Winterson, Jeanette (1996) Art Objects, p. 178).

Index